Mel Hensey

Continuous Excellence

Building Effective Organizations

A HANDBOOK FOR MANAGERS AND LEADERS

Published by
ASCE Press
American Society of Civil Engineers
345 East 47th Street
New York, New York 10017-2398

ABSTRACT:

This handbook for managers and leaders pulls together, in one resource, all that is important to know about effectively utilizing and managing change in service organizations. For leaders and managers at every level, change has become the number one necessity and headache. Employees also feel the impacts of change in service organizations. This book addresses both traditional approaches to change, such as strategic planning and new methods like re-engineering. Every important management facet or responsibility is addressed, from getting the work, to doing it well, to getting paid. It is truly a handbook for managers who want to advance their organization to the next level of performance excellence.

Library of Congress Cataloging-in-Publication Data

Hensey, Mel.
    Continuous excellence : building effective organizations / Mel Hensey.
        p.   cm.
    Includes index.
    ISBN 0-7844-0013-X
       1. Industrial management. 2. Organizational change—Management.3.
    Organizational effectiveness. 4. Industrial management—Employee partici
    pation.   I. Title.
    HD31.H4723 1995   95-33580
    658.4—dc20   CIP

ANOTHER BOOK BY THE AUTHOR

Collective Excellence: Building Effective Teams, 1992
... available through ASCE Press

THE AIM OF THIS HANDBOOK

For leaders and managers at every level, **change** has become the number one necessity and headache. They must wrestle with runaway technology, heaps of risk and regulation as well as opportunity!

This **Handbook for Managers and Leaders** pulls together, in one resource, all that's important to know about effectively utilizing and managing **change** in this turbulent time.

In this Handbook, we try to address all the tricky issues of leading and managing **necessary change** while creating continuous excellence and renewal for all types of service organizations.

The book addresses both **traditional** approaches to change, such as strategic planning and **new methods** like re-engineering. Every important management facet or responsibility is addressed, from getting the work, to doing it well, to getting paid.

As one reviewer noted, it is truly a handbook for managers who want to advance their organization to the next level of performance excellence. And one that does it in a simple, clear, concise way available nowhere else!

As process consultants, we aim to respect, focus, and optimize our clients' own wisdom, creativity and information ... as opposed to telling them "how to" solve problems or "how to" grasp opportunities (as if we knew how!).

With this in mind, *CONTINUOUS EXCELLENCE* is a book mostly about **PROCESSES** — processes that will almost always lead to improvement, and ultimately to excellence!

ABOUT THE AUTHOR

Melville Hensey is Carol Hensey's partner in their consulting firm in Cincinnati. Their work focuses on helping organizations, public or private, with major change and improvement efforts such as:

- Culture change.
- Strategic planning.
- Organization redesign.
- Continuous improvement.
- Creative conflict resolution.
- Organizational effectiveness.
- Organizational problem solving.
- Management Team development.

Mel enjoyed working in technical organizations as an engineer and manager, before he and Carol formed their consulting group in 1974. His work in Earth Science Labs (consulting), Cincinnati Bell (construction) and Procter & Gamble (engineering) provided the practical experience needed to serve his clients' needs.

Clients with whom the Henseys have recently worked include Woodward-Clyde Consultants, Black & Veatch Engineers, Ferro Corporation, Civil Engineering Research Foundation, Ohio State University, Miami University, the IEEE, Atkinson Construction, The American Society of Civil Engineers, U.S. Army Corps of Engineers, Stanley Consultants and Greiner Engineering.

Mel served as faculty for several management institutes including the Construction Executive Program of Texas A&M University and the Executive Effectiveness Course of the American Management Association.

As founding editor of ASCE's *Journal of Management in Engineering*, he guided it through its first six years, developing the "Management Forum" to enable practitioners more easily to share management tools and argue issues, earning ASCE's Torrens award.

Carol and Mel live in Cincinnati, where they stay in touch with their four children and six grandchildren. They enjoy travel, canoeing, tree planting, volunteer work, and grandbabysitting. Over the years and still today, their firm has a family team flavor:

Mel, Sr.: principal consultant and salesperson.

Carol: communication, office and financial manager.

Mel, Jr.: our financial and computer consultant.

Ann: secretarial services provider (her own firm).

ACKNOWLEDGMENTS
and
APPRECIATIONS

This book is dedicated to Carol, my wife, friend and business partner. Carol continues to be a quiet mainstay in serving our Hensey Associates clients well and in supporting me while I'm on the road.

In their own unique way, each of our grown children have contributed to this work. Mel, Terry, Chris and Ann, have shared powerful insights about what makes organizations work well, based on their own interests, work experiences and keen observations.

I appreciate many of the important basics of organization effectiveness learned 20 to 35 years ago in the Engineering Division of Procter & Gamble: Basics such as group process, personnel selection and client feedback are only recently being fully appreciated by many firms.

I'm also indebted to many creative clients that we serve in our organizational effectiveness consulting work. These executives, some of whom have been clients for 10 to 20 years, have contributed to our learnings directly and through very challenging assignments. Many of them are heroes to me. For example ...

One of the oldest clients we have is Lockwood, Jones & Beals: Engineers & Architects, founded by Bill Lockwood. Not satisfied with starting a major mid-west consulting firm, Bill has also created an enterprise to license his breakthrough development, **Con/Span**, a precast arch bridge with many applications.

I'm also grateful to the "Hound of Heaven" described in Francis Thompson's wonderful poem about the Lord of Life, who is still hounding me (in His caring way) to be useful. I hope this book may prove to be useful to you and those in your organization, as you provide **needed** services in the **spirit** of service, striving for **Continuous Excellence**.

Sincerely,

Mel Hensey, P.E., F.ASCE

CONTENTS

FOREWORD

We are living and working in a period of jarring change that grows more unpredictable, and sometimes more perilous, every day. Tofler's book *Future Shock* (published by Random House, 1970) gave us dire warnings of this.

Visionary consultants are suggesting that we have entered into a period of unpredictable and discontinuous change not seen for 500 years or more. Peter Vaill calls it continuous turbulence with no place to regroup. Imparato and Harari speak of "jumping the curve" in their book by that name. **Whatever** it is ... it **is** challenging!

Recent work by Proudfoot Change Management, reported in *Business Week* for September 20, 1993, found that American businesses are changing with the times, but aren't happy about it:

- Almost 80% report change in their companies is rapid.

- More than 60% say they approach change less than eagerly and they expect the rate of change to increase.

- More than 50% believe their firms are not capable of coping with change.

- Fewer than 50% have formal means of handling change.

Three different observers ... Albert Einstein, Buckminster Fuller and Tony Frank (former postmaster general and CEO of First Nationwide Bank) ... have made a very similar observation:

> The kind and quality of thinking required to deal with the problems of our times will need to be much better than the thinking that has gotten us into these problems!

My hopes for this handbook include helping the managers of service organizations to be **continuously effective** in the face of accelerating change.

An increasing percentage of managers' work is the **management** of change, but even more than that, it's **creating** change wherever needed in their project, unit, division, office, service area, firm or agency.

And, increasingly, **employees** at all levels expect to contribute by helping to create more effective systems, processes and tasks so that their everyday work is more effective and satisfying.

This book is intended to be a help to managing and participating in **change focused on improvement** for executives, managers and staffs.

CHAPTER 1

JARRING AND TURBULENT CHANGE

Peter Vaill, writing in *Management as a Performing Art*, talks about the shift to continuous and turbulent change ... which is and will be with us. The future will reward organizations with the vision and leadership to deal with and to create the necessary change to maintain **continuous** excellence.

This is the normal business curve for products, services and organizations (when they don't continuously re-invent themselves).

Maturity

Some of America's business giants are now on this side of the curve!

Growth   Decline

Birth   Death

Time

Figure 1

To stay on the "growth" side of the normal business curve requires ...

- clear vision.
- risk-taking.
- leadership.
- creating new markets.
- creating new services.
- **continuous** excellence.

Peter Drucker observed that progress isn't made by solving problems so much as it is made by grasping **opportunities** when they present themselves.

Searching for Silver Bullets

It's gotten to be confusing and frustrating just to open the mail these days! From every point of the compass, executives and managers are bombarded by the latest in how to get ahead of the competition.

Both Peter Drucker and Edwards Deming have noted and commented on the rapidly evolving plethora of management systems, cure-alls, magic bullets and salvations.

A recent article in June 1994 ***Management Review*** (published by American Management Association) is cleverly titled: "The Boss Has Read Another New Book!" (so look for **another** new program, initiative or corporate culture).

Here's a recent batch of new management approaches I'm aware of:

- Core Competencies.
- Cross-Functional Teams.
- Quality Function Deployment.
- Business Process Re-Engineering.
- Re-inventing the Organization.
- Next Operation as Customer.
- Reducing Cycle Times.
- Strategic Management.
- Employee Empowerment.
- Just-In-Time Training.
- Partial Quality Management.
- Open-Book Management.
- 360-Degree Feedback.

All of the new concepts or approaches are excellent. However ...

1. Most of them are fundamental aspects and basic parts of **any** effective organization.

2. They are **interdependent** and inseparable from one another, not stand-alone systems.

3. Some management consulting and training organizations like to highlight theirs as **the** most important, and name it the "_____ system or program."

2

Taking a Systems View

Managers and consultants who have a general systems view of organizations tend not to get caught in this trap of the "one best way." They ...

- **Learn** about, develop and broaden their understandings of organizational effectiveness.

- **Focus** on the need for increased effectiveness in particular areas of their organization.

- **Plan** for organizational improvement carefully, because they realize systems change requires good work in several areas:

  - attitudes   - skills   - knowledge - practices
  - processes   - linkages   - systems   - procedures

- **Utilize** change management approaches that work, including:

  - leading visibly and credibly with clear vision and goals.

  - providing effective education and training (realizing most of it is poorly done).

  - following up changes with the necessary fine-tuning.

  - supporting changes with their evaluation, review, reward and recognition systems.

  - setting the example by changing their own behaviors.

- **Avoid** the fad trap, but they use everything that makes sense.

- **View** all important functions as a system that needs to work together.

- **Maintain** "constancy of purpose" in their priorities and communication.

Over-reliance on Failed Methods

On the other hand, executives and owners do sometimes get a sense that they should or would like to develop their organizations to be more effective in some particular way.

Sometimes this "itch" is a result of their observation that they are under-performing in terms of profitability, market share, clients won and lost, employee morale and results, and so on.

Other times, it may come from a formal survey of employees, clients, managers or some combination. Or, from a peer review or management conference.

In the new world of "Continuous Excellence," owners and executives who are serious about long term competitiveness ... will view organization development as **continuously** necessary for all units, top to bottom.

Our consulting experiences suggest that many leaders and managers have far too much faith in the customary, most used, most traditional approaches:

- Training   • Re-structuring   • Management memo

- **Training**, according to research by the American Quality Foundation (New York, NY) as well as our own observations, can be and usually is enormously wasteful and relatively ineffective. The reasons are many, but certainly include these:

  - The content of the training is not modeled (walked) by management, nor supported by supervision.

  - Most human behavior is habitual and hard to change. Most "training" doesn't recognize that fact and lacks the elements required to help people internalize new habits of behavior.

- **Re-structuring**, whether in the form of fine-tuning or major overhaul, often leads to mass confusion in the ranks, at least initially, because of ...

  - lack of clarity about the **new** roles.

  - lack of management support and/or training.

  - little help with problem solving in the implementation work.

  The results are almost always lost productivity in the early days; sometimes it's never recaptured! Significant structural changes can take up to three years to be integrated.

- **Management memos** are important communication tools. When used to emphasize a point, introduce a theme or support **other** forms of communication, they can be effective. However, they suffer from ...

  - lack of staff discussion and feedback.

  - unintended consequences through misinterpretation.

  - overly re-focused priorities.

  - endless scuttlebutt over "what it means."

An Integrated Path to Excellence

While all three of these approaches have a place and can be done well, today's leaders and managers in service firms and agencies **need more**.

The rest of this book will try to suggest and define some of the **best** ways to develop organizations in **many** important areas. Most of this we have gratefully learned from our clients and colleagues, as well as practical management writers.

Aspects of organization development offered in these pages will address ...

- Roles of Leadership and Management
- Learning from Clients and Customers
- Guideposts Every Employee Needs
- Strategic Planning and Implementation
- Continuous Improvement and TQM
- Benchmarking: Easy and Necessary
- Business Process Re-engineering
- Managing Your Culture Change
- Starting New Offices, Services, Business Units
- Developing and Using Teams
- Partnerships and Alliances
- Communication and Excellence
- Secrets of Project Management
- Meetings that Really Get Work Done
- Strengthening the Staffing Function
- Managers Have to Be Facilitators
- Relationships that Get Results
- Using the Past as Future Guide

... and more.

CHAPTER 2

MANAGEMENT IS NOT LEADERSHIP

Leadership and management **are** different, no question about that. And **both** are needed in most organizations. There have been some interesting, perhaps even useful, distinctions made between leadership and management. Here are several of my favorites:

Leadership	Management
• Guiding by example.	• Guiding by control.
• Concerned with effectiveness.	• Concerned with efficiency.
• Interested in change.	• Interested in stability.
• Doing the right things.	• Doing things right.
• Anyone can exhibit leadership.	• Managers are usually appointed.

Clearly, we need most of these, and so we need **both** leaders **and** managers!

Thirty-five Important Abilities

We've often been asked to help clients identify these abilities in a bit more detail, specifically enough to be useful for assessment, or for training and development. This is our list as it has developed so far:

1. Finding/hiring talented staff.
2. Choosing excellent, challenging people.
3. Evaluating strengths and weaknesses.
4. Setting a developmental climate for staff.
5. Confronting problem subordinates.

6. Appreciating and valuing diversity.
7. Creating/working in a team orientation.
8. Facilitating/leading meetings well.
9. Utilizing strengths and abilities of others.
10. Getting results when not "in charge."

11. Self-awareness and understanding.

12. Compassion and sensitivity to others.

13. Composure under difficult conditions.

14. Humility and sense of humor.

15. Self-renewal and development.

16. Open, straight-forward communication.

17. Trustworthy; able to inspire trust.

18. Putting people at ease; rapport.

19. Building and mending relationships.

20. Able to negotiate in and for the group.

21. Decisive when and as appropriate.

22. Resourcefulness in solving problems.

23. Doing whatever it takes; perseverance.

24. Acting with flexibility; not rigid.

25. Positive "can do" attitude.

26. Technical knowledge of the business.

27. Customer and quality system knowledge.

28. Knowing how to use systems to manage.

29. Entrepreneurship; developing the "business."

30. Managing the financials successfully.

31. Effectively leading others.

32. Leading through mission, vision, values.

33. Involving others in setting the goals.

34. Being visible and available; MBWA (management by walking around).

35. Establishing "authority" by earning it.

We've "collected" our list from our own experience and have also been helped by the works of: The Association for Creative Change, Lombardo and McCauley, Ichak Adizes, Warren Bennis, as well as Cannie and Caplin.

Now obviously some of these detailed abilities are more **leadership** and some are more **management**. But some of them are both and some are neither. For example, 11 through 19 have to do with understanding and managing oneself, or just basic communication. (Perhaps they should be listed first!)

Greenleaf's Perspective

There may be more books around and emerging on "leadership" than any other topic. However, one of the best is *Servant Leadership* by Robert K. Greenleaf (published by Paulist Press, 1977). It's become a classic and is even more appreciated as it ages.

Greenleaf's notion is being adopted by service firms small and large, such as Schneider Engineering Company, Indianapolis, and delivery giant Federal Express.

Greenleaf was the leader of organization development for AT&T for many years. His perspectives are practical and come out of the experiences of real work, not theory.

Learning from Lincoln

Don Phillips has written a provocative view of President Lincoln as a leader from whom current leaders may learn a lot in *Lincoln on Leadership* (published by Warner Books, 1992). Phillips noted that though many have written about Lincoln's life and presidency, almost nothing exists as to Lincoln the **Leader**! Phillips regards Lincoln as "the greatest leader this country, and perhaps this world, has yet known."

Lincoln was a leader who understood and used the concept of MBWA, even though it was far more difficult for him than it is for most modern-day leaders. His personal secretaries, Hay and Nicolay, noted that Lincoln would see as many people as often as he possibly could and was one of the most accessible chief executives the United States has ever known.

Throughout the war Lincoln visited his generals and men in the field and when he couldn't, he either ...

- spent time at the telegraph office, or
- sent special emissaries to the front.

He also took time to visit hospitals where wounded soldiers were recuperating. Phillips also notes that Lincoln called on Congress regularly and was the first president in many years to attend a regular working session of the Senate.

Lincoln knew that **frequent human contact** was essential in creating a sense of ...

- Commitment,
- Collaboration,
- Community,

... and to exchange vital information so necessary in making timely and effective decisions.

Quality Leadership

Jacqueline Miller, reporting on research by the American Quality Foundation at the 1993 conference on "Restoring America's Leadership," had some tips for managers interested in improving leadership for their organizations:

- Recognize that American culture is different from others.
- Americans generally want to improve themselves.
- People need specific and immediate feedback in order to improve.
- Value and use the cultural diversity of our workers.
- Encourage and take seriously employee ideas for improvement.
- Promote a risk-taking environment where people learn from mistakes.
- Provide support for continuous learning by all.
- Recognize success and achievement soon and often.

Leader as Facilitator

Our own view is that leaders need all the preceding, plus a whole new set of skills. That "new" set is commonly called **facilitating** and is aimed at enabling a group to do its best work, through:

- Awareness of **process** (**how** work is done, not **what** is done).
- Ability to hear and synthesize what **others** are saying.
- **Meeting** leadership skills, from the meeting's purpose through to the documentation.
- Options to help a group get **un**stuck when it's off-track or frustrated.
- Skills for turning the inevitable conflicts into **agreements** (the problem-solver "win/win" style).

I was fortunate to work for several facilitating type leaders/managers, in construction, engineering and human resource work. In these days of the "professional facilitator," I see many who are ineffective and need to learn a lot about the five skill sets listed above.

CHAPTER 3

WHAT CLIENTS AND CUSTOMERS WANT

Effective organizations must, **above all else**, remain well focused on **whom** they exist to **serve**!

Universal Wants

Inspired by many clients and customer service researchers, we developed this list of things almost all customers and clients universally want:

- Being accessible when they need you!
- Knowing and responding to their needs.
- Knowledge (expertise) about your business.
- Keeping promises (under-promise, over-deliver).
- Being prompt in all service aspects.
- Information, both basic and updates.
- Getting it right the first time every time.
- Fixing it, if necessary, quickly and well.
- Reasonable cost for the benefits you provide.
- Creativity as appropriate to the situation.
- Relating with personal rapport and respect.

And, there's no such thing as "satisfaction," only degrees of satisfaction. In other words, Good is better than Satisfactory, but not up to Excellent, and way below Delightful. And still better is to provide desired features the client didn't know he/she needed!

When all the hubbub dies out, perhaps the greatest contributions of Total Quality Management (TQM) to organizations may turn out to be these:

- Re-discovery of the importance of working closely with one's customers, clients, and users.
- Recognition by public service organizations that they, too, are customer-driven if they want to survive.
- Discovery that one's internal colleagues and sister units are also "customers" in that they must often use the results of our work.
- Customers, clients and users are the very best sources of quality measures and even ideas for improvement.

Costs of Quality

Many writers have addressed the so-called "costs of quality." Actually, in many cases, these could be better labeled the costs of **un**-quality! Here's a sampler of these costs, that represents a broad spectrum of service organizations:

- Re-do's, retro-fits, call-backs, wasted effort.
- Unpaid bills, claims, payments, litigation.
- Lost (future) sales.
- Poor employee morale; frustration.
- Lost reputation and lost sales.

True costs of quality would be **investments** which do indeed contribute to quality and to client satisfaction, such as:

- Process improvements.
- Training and development.
- Better, faster and cheaper service.
- New services or features.

What Clients Want from Consulting Engineers

John Urban, CEO of Edwards & Kelcey, Inc., of Livingston, New Jersey, provided us with these highlights of client perceptions of consulting engineers, from a study conducted for the American Consulting Engineers Council (ACEC).

Clients gave high ratings to technically oriented issues, such as:

- Ability to understand technical issues.
- Providing expertise not available in-house.
- Conforming to performance standards.
- Designing constructable projects.
- Providing objective, unbiased recommendations.
- Ability to identify and diagnose problems.
- Design completeness and accuracy.

Much lower ratings were received from clients on business-related skills, such as these:

- Ability to meet time schedules.
- Ability to stay within budget.

11

- Ability to communicate with non-technical people.
- Providing senior management project supervision.
- Service during a project (design and construction).
- Service after project completion.

They also recommend that we:

- Improve communications with clients.
- Provide more education and continuing education for engineers.

What Clients Want from Environmental Firms

Rich Millet, Chief Practice Officer of Woodward-Clyde Consultants in Denver, Colorado, undertook an in-depth focus group with several large corporate clients, seeking specific feedback on their services. The following recommendations come from that effort, as well as similar focus groups for other engineering and environmental service firms.

- **Client's Needs and Expectations:**
  - Thorough discovery process (up front).
  - Documentation of scope for project teams.
  - Contract terms reflect real agreements with client.
  - Surveying client's perception of job completion and satisfaction.

- **Communication During Projects:**
  - Regular client updates on the project.
  - Effective internal project team communication.
  - Candor in reporting/discussing issues.
  - Representing the client well to regulators.
  - Few (nasty) surprises; quick handling of problems.

- **Quality of Studies and Reports:**
  - Well written; no need to re-do.
  - Clear graphics; helpful to regulators.
  - Timely; arrive in time to review first.
  - Represents client well to regulators.
  - Examines alternative remedies for situation.
  - Involves client in selection of best solution.
  - Cost estimates with appropriate ranges.
  - Solution-focus vs. technical-focus.
  - Considers impact on client's budget.

- **Quality of Specifications and Drawings, if any:**
  - Well organized, easy to follow and use.
  - Either standard or custom; but not cobbled together.
  - Drawing graphics clear and simple; not overdone.
  - Compatible with client's CAD system if appropriate.
  - Timely; arrive in time to review and stay on schedule.
  - No/few errors, omissions or interferences.
  - "Seamless"; well coordinated between disciplines.
  - Constructable without contractor re-design.

- **Invoicing for Completed Work:**
  - Accuracy in completed work, including carry-forward.
  - Includes necessary documentation and backup.
  - No surprises for extra work, or other problems.

- **Project Wrap-up and Critique:**
  - Get client's feedback on the degree to which expectations were met.
  - Find out how well regarded you were in terms of ...
    - Quality of working relationships?
    - How do we compare to competitors?
    - Would you use our firm again?
    - Would you recommend us to others?

These views were provided by private sector clients including Xerox, Chevron, Procter & Gamble, Union Pacific, Kroger, Weyerhaeuser, IBM and General Motors.

What Do Your Customers Want?

There are four basic ways to get helpful and specific feedback and input from your clients or customers.

First, and most importantly, elicit feedback during the time of proposing-negotiating-contracting-delivering the service. We recently did a survey of engineering and environmental service firms. Following are some "headlines" about expectations **their** clients have:

- Listening to and understanding the client. Developing a clear understanding of client quality expectations. Know what the client wants and is willing to pay for.

13

- Possessing and applying technical skill. Providing staff with the training and tools necessary for delivering required quality product. Understanding the construction process.

- Listening to and understanding the client. Obtaining continuous feedback from clients to **assess** how we are performing. Are the expectations being met?

Second most important is the opportunity for in-depth feedback at the end of project or service delivery. Some firms call this the "project post-mortem." More firms talk about it than actually do it. That's unfortunate because it can convey the message that we **really** care! Not only that, but a high percentage of times, it may lead to new work!

Third, are client focus groups: Here the client group may represent one client or several who have similar needs and interests in a particular type of facility or service. Such meetings should be well planned, well led, well focused and supported so that clients' time is clearly appreciated. These meetings have value over other methods because clients can be very specific, can interact with one another and the service-provider.

Several firms have gotten so tuned-in to their clients that they regard them as "partners," with the level of trust, interaction, frequent communication and honesty that partnership implies. Interestingly, several firms feel they have a better working relationship with some **clients** than they do with other parts of their **own** firm!

Finally, there are surveys, whether by phone or by mail, done in-company or by an "outside" survey service. Whoever designs and does the survey, it needs to be simple, brief, well organized, and personalized (sent to a specific individual) to be taken seriously. Several sample surveys are enclosed, courtesy of our clients, in **Figures 3, 4 and 5**.

At their best, surveys should be a part of an ongoing dialogue with clients, where we ask for their help and then let them know what we learned and how we plan to use it!

Perhaps the most effective, and certainly the simplest **feedback survey process** comes from consulting colleague Melody Jones of St. Louis who attributes it to ODI of Burlington, Massachusetts.

The process involves asking your clients what **they** view as important about your services or products. The preamble or focus statement can be broad or narrow as necessary.

The key feature here is that the client doesn't get steered into questions he/she doesn't really care about! No assumptions need be made.

These questions are best asked by phone but we've discovered they also work by mail. As part of that process, ask **how important** it is (1 to 10; 10 is high) and **how we're doing** (1 to 10) on that item!

Figure 2 provides a simple format for recording client responses.

Person Interviewed: _____

by: _____ **date:** _____

Something they view as important in **your product or service**	**Level of importance?** **(1-10)**
	How are we doing? **(1-10)**

Person Interviewed: _____

by: _____ **date:** ___ _____

Something they view as important in **your product or service**	**Level of importance?** **(1-10)**
	How are we doing? **(1-10)**

Person Interviewed: _____

by: _____ **date:** _____

Something they view as important in **your product or service**	**Level of importance?** **(1-10)**
	How are we doing? **(1-10)**

Figure 2

HOW DID YOU FIND OUR SERVICE?

	OVERALL	ARCHITECTURAL	SURVEY	CIVIL	STRUCTURAL
	5 4 3 2 1	5 4 3 2 1	5 4 3 2 1	5 4 3 2 1	5 4 3 2 1
PERCEPTION OF YOUR NEEDS					
RESPONSIVENESS					
TECHNICAL COMPETENCE					
SOLUTIONS					
COST EFFECTIVENESS (PROJECT)					
VALUE FOR FEE PAID					

COMMENT _____

RATING:
5 - Excellent   4 - Good   3 - Average
2 - Fair   1 - Poor

HOW WERE WE TO DO BUSINESS WITH?

	5 4 3 2 1
PROJECT MANAGEMENT	
SUPPORT STAFF (TELEPHONE, ETC.)	
ACCOUNTING	

COMMENT _____

WOULD YOU USE/RECOMMEND OUR FIRM FOR ANOTHER PROJECT?   ☐ YES   ☐ NO

COMMENT _____

DO YOU BELIEVE THAT THE LEVEL OF OUR SERVICE IS:

☐ IMPROVING   ☐ SLIPPING   ☐ UNCHANGED   ☐ N/A

WE WOULD APPRECIATE ANY COMMENTS ABOUT YOUR EXPERIENCE WITH OUR FIRM AND ANY IDEAS THAT COULD HELP IMPROVE OUR SERVICE. IF ANY MEMBERS OF OUR STAFF WERE ESPECIALLY HELPFUL AND RESPONSIVE TO YOUR NEEDS, PLEASE INCLUDE THEIR NAME/NAMES SO THAT WE CAN RECOGNIZE THEIR EFFORTS.

COMMENT _____

NAME OF PROJECT _____   DATE _____

NAME OF COMPANY _____   SIGNATURE _____

Dear Client:

Please take a few minutes to fill out and return this evaluation card (postage prepaid). It is important to us to learn about your experiences with our firm. Your feedback will help improve our service.

Also, if you would like to discuss anything concerning your project, please feel free to call me. Our phone number is (513) 293-6967.

Thank you,

Bill

W.D. Lockwood

Note: Refold card with our address on outside.

Figure 3: Sample Client Survey

16

Corporate Research

Inorganic Materials Group

Division:		Not satisfied				Well satisfied
Were we available when you needed to contact us?		1	2	3	4	5
Comments:						
If we were not, did we get back to you soon enough?		1	2	3	4	5
Comments:						
Did we understand your needs well?		1	2	3	4	5
Comments:						
Did we address your needs in a timely manner?		1	2	3	4	5
Comments:						
Did we address your needs with work of expected quality?		1	2	3	4	5
Comments:						
Did we keep you informed of our progress?		1	2	3	4	5
Comments:						
Did we exhibit organization and thoughtfulness in our efforts?		1	2	3	4	5
Comments:						
Did we work well with you as a team?		1	2	3	4	5
Comments:						

We strive for continual improvement in our work.
How can we do what we do better?

Please send to:
          Corporate Research

Figure 4: Sample Client Survey

Name:_____Title:___ _____

Company/Agency Name:_____

Phone Number:_____Date:_____

WE WOULD APPRECIATE YOUR FEEDBACK!

Your satisfaction is important. Please take a moment to complete this evaluation and let us know how well we are serving you on the following project/task:

Project/Task:_____

W-C Project Manager:_____Date:_____

	Did Not Meet Expectations	Met Expectations	Exceeded Expectations
Value of Our Service			
Staying on Schedule			
Listening to and Understanding Your Needs and Maintaining Communications			
Responding to Your Requests			
Providing Solutions to Your Needs			
Project/Task Budget Management			

Overall Project/Task Performance
(Mark with an "x")

Poor			Satisfactory						Excellent
1	2	3	4	5	6	7	8	9	10

For Similar Services, Where Would You
Benchmark W-C Compared to Our Competitors
(Mark with an "x")

Lower Qtr.	3rd Qtr.	2nd Qtr.	Top Qtr.

Additional Comments:_____

_____

_____

_____

Please return this card in the enclosed, self-addressed postage-paid envelope or feel free to contact:

Richard A. Millet
Chief Practice Officer
Woodward-Clyde
4582 South Ulster Street, Suite 600
Denver, CO 80237
1-800-755-6987, ext. 3959

Thank you for responding.

Figure 5: Sample Client Survey

18

CHAPTER 4

MARKETING, SALES, BUSINESS DEVELOPMENT

In the service areas of research, consulting, design, planning, environmental, engineering and construction, the business of securing work assignments seems to be misunderstood by many employees.

There are some traditional marketing approaches that ought to work but often **don't**. Yet there are some non-traditional avenues for getting work that often **do** work. Let's explore some of each.

We often hear a lot of argument about the differences between marketing, sales and business development. But the term "getting the work" seems to cover all three very nicely.

Getting the work is, in a very real way, part of every step of the project or service delivery cycle. We've tried to show this for a research, consulting, design or construction organization in **Figure 6**.

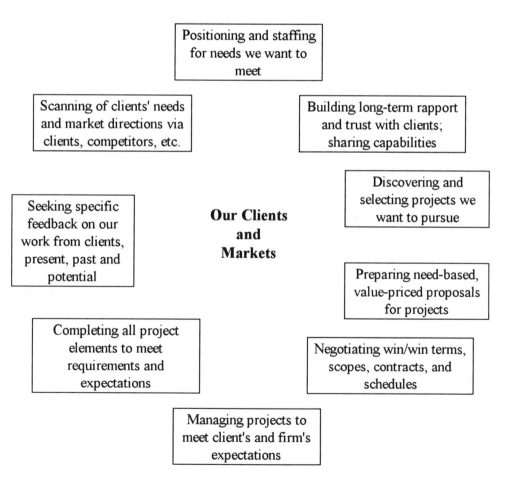

Figure 6: The Marketing/Sales/Performance Cycle

Harvey Kaye, writing in *Inside the Technical Consulting Business* (a Wiley-Interscience Publication, 1994), believes there are "Three fundamental truths of technical marketing." Perhaps there are more than three, but his three nominations certainly deserve mention here:

- There is a genuine need for the services we're offering.
- **Getting the work is more difficult than doing the work.**
- It's easier and less competitive to win work early in the life cycle of a particular service.

Actually, we believe there are only three basic parts to any service business (or agency!):

- **Developing** (and keeping) clients.
- **Performing** their work well.
- **Getting** paid for it!

Impact of the Life Cycle

Many marketers over the years have sketched the so-called "Life Cycle" of products, services, even organizations, as they go through: Birth, growth, maturity and decline (and sometimes death).

Table 1 provides a look at this **life cycle** from a **marketing and sales** standpoint, with some comments and strategies appropriate for each stage.

Table 1: Marketing/Sales Stages

"Birthing" Stage	"Pioneer" Stage	"Me-too" Stage	"Commodity" Stage
Requires investment: - People - Tools - Software - Promotion	Requires value-pricing to recoup the investment and earn **strong** profits.	Competition leads to tighter pricing and therefore requires differentiation for **good** profits.	Bidding and cutthroat pricing leads to the need for a price-based strategy for **any** profits. P.S. - It's time to re-invent it!

Guidelines for Getting the Work

Following are some of the basic necessities of business development for providers of technical services, be they studies, design, research, engineering, planning, development of alternatives, construction, or whatever!

1. Get to know clients (or prospects) **very** well, both as business-people and personalities with families, hobbies, problems and life outside of work.

    Harvey Mackay of "Swim with the Sharks" fame, has a list of 66 questions he uses to get really acquainted with a client. But we really don't need his list, we should develop our **own** list!

2. Recognize that almost all **effective** business development and sales work is done ...

    *   at the **personal** level by individuals, not by organizations.

    *   at the **professional** and supervisory level, not by executives.

    *   more often by the **technical** people, not by sales people.

3. Conduct research, gather resources, and do self-development that leads to ...

    *   having **unique** information and approaches.

    *   being a **true** expert and needed resource.

    However, remember: **nobody** likes a smart-ass; don't **sound** like an expert!

4. Send out information that benefits clients (or prospects) on a frequent basis. However, be sure that it is ...

    *   frequent, simple and brief.

    *   useful and interesting from the **client's** perspective!

    *   **not** self-promotional.

5. Get published, give talks, attend functions, host seminars where **clients** (or prospects) are; not just colleagues (or competitors).

    This would suggest users' groups and associations are more valuable than professional societies.

21

6. Work hard to speak to clients in their language with **their** needs and interests in mind more so than what we are trying to sell, offer, market or explain.

   This is a lot easier to do if we are **listening** more than speaking.

7. Bring in key people from clients' (or prospects') organizations and industry to talk to the staff. David Maister calls this a "reverse seminar."

   This can provide unique "training" as well as a linkage into key client contacts and networks.

8. Recognize differences in individuals. Clients frequently have significant personal style differences, motivational differences, different values and certainly different goals from their consultants.

   It's vital to know how the world makes sense to clients and respond to their needs and goals in that context.

9. During a project, **over**-communicate with clients. This doesn't suggest verbosity or long reports. It means **frequently**.

   Strive for "no surprises"; always provide early notice of difficulties, unusual circumstances, etc. quickly, as well as steps being taken to manage the situation.

10. Learn and use the simple communication tools for establishing **rapport**. Scientists and engineers sometimes view rapport with suspicion. All humans subconsciously respond to rapport or react to its absence.

    Rapport includes responding to the other person's ...

    - pace or rhythm.

    - posture and gestures.

    - emotional tone, etc.

11. As part of the regular and frequent communication with clients, seek specific **feedback and suggestions** from them by way of ...

    - plant or site visits.

    - follow-ups on interim reports.

    - surveys once or twice a year.

- asking at several levels.
- project post-mortems.

12. Note carefully those already in the organization who are great at business development. They do many of these things instinctively and well. They also ...

   - almost always do more than is expected; they **add extra value**.
   - work as if everything depended on them, but also seek and use help.
   - see themselves as sort of self-employed; that is, they behave like owners.

13. Watch those great business developers as they interact with clients; note their words, gestures, posture, timing, voice tone, hesitations, etc.

   Try to determine their successful strategies (strategies they are probably unaware of).

14. In addition to responding to requests, RFQ's or RFP's, be willing to take the initiative and develop proposals that will/may address needs that clients do or will have.

   If funding is or will be a problem, propose unique approaches that will address that issue.

15. Maintain close and frequent contact with significant clients after project completion; be the first to know when new needs are emerging.

   Some call this "wiring" the project but it's just good, up-front business development work.

16. The future belongs to those who strive to do their work better, faster **and** cheaper.

   In other words, those who aim for **continuous excellence**, never resting on their laurels or successes.

   Edwards Deming noted that there's no law stating that anyone has to improve. It's optional. It's only a matter of survival.

17. Use benchmarking, a part of Total Quality Management, for a systematic approach to assessing how we're doing compared to the **same** functions in other respected organizations.

   This will become a greater necessity in the future as we strive to improve and learn from the best.

18. Respect and preserve **existing** clients in every way possible; retaining a client requires one tenth the energy of winning a new one.

   Effective consulting and research organizations know that client retention is crucial and consider 90% repeat work a high level of performance. Yet, existing clients are often taken for granted.

19. In many situations the **best** business developers are **existing** clients ... as they comment on, refer, or complain to others.

   Someone who has **used** your services is often a far more objective and credible information source about your service than anyone else!

20. Realize that a failure or problem, large or small, presents an unusual marketing opportunity.

   Research shows that under these conditions, if you work hard to **recover**, the client will be both **more** satisfied and appreciative than if there were **no** problems at all.

21. Take the risk of talking with clients you have lost or fear you may lose. They have things to tell you that may be very helpful.

   If this is done with good listening and sincerity, you also have a chance to regain them (if you want to).

First developed for
the Research Division of the Ferro Corporation

We've recently come across a unique, practical and helpful resource called *The "I Hate Selling" Book* by Allan S. Boress (published by AMACOM, New York, NY, 1995). In it, Allan provides good business-building advice for consultants, attorneys, engineers, scientists, architects and other professional service providers!

CHAPTER 5

GUIDEPOSTS EVERY EMPLOYEE NEEDS

Whether an organization is in need of a little process improvement, a strategic plan, a structural overhaul or re-engineering from scratch, all employees need and deserve some basic **guideposts** to orient and focus their work.

Individuals need them ... groups need them ... and leaders most certainly need them. Here are the guideposts most often discussed and found useful in organizations of all kinds.

Basic Business

This is a simple statement of what we do in the world that people or organizations need or want. Here are some examples:

- Consulting Engineering.
- Higher Education.
- Nursing Care.
- Contract Manufacturing.
- Environmental Science.
- Construction.
- Corrections.
- Entertainment.

Unique/Core Competencies

How do we approach our Basic Business? What is our distinct advantage? What is our recipe for success at our Basic Business? What are our **core** competencies that set us apart from competitors? Here is a sampling:

- Lowest Cost.
- Customer-Driven.
- Innovative Solutions.
- Customization.
- Absolute Reliability.
- Most Responsive.
- Market Dominance.
- State of the Art.

While it's likely that there may be several drivers to a business, usually one will be paramount. Protecting that advantage and/or competency(ies) and keeping it sharp is even more important!

Mission or Purpose

Mission defines our purpose, main objective, calling, the reason for the existence of our organization. It expresses our distinctive competence and/or unique contribution to those we serve.

To be effective, a mission needs to be clear, specific, brief, dynamic and current. **Everyone** in the organization needs to know and support the mission. For that to happen, the mission should be memorable and inspiring!

Sometimes a management group will tell me that they have a current mission statement, but no one can remember it! That's like **not** having one.

> **Example:** To be the environmental consultant of choice in our selected markets.

Core Values

All organizations have values and usually lots of them. Sometimes they are explicit, but mostly they are discovered by accidentally bumping up against one of them! Many firms have found it useful to discuss and identify the few **"core" values** that seem to be truly essential to corporate success.

> **Examples:**
> - Integrity and honesty, both inside and outside the firm.
> - Never too busy to assist a team member in need.

Vision

Vision differs significantly from mission! Our vision defines a clear picture of what we aim to be at some stated time in the future. It expresses what we'll be doing, seeing and creating, in concrete, specific terms.

A clear vision is important because whatever we can collectively visualize, with feeling, we can achieve.

> **Example:** The vision of the Administrative Services and Information Technologies Division is that it will, on a continuously improving basis, be a pre-eminent, non-academic service unit in the nation, delivering agreed-upon levels of service in a highly efficient, effective and innovative manner that builds user satisfaction and worker pride.

The development of a clear vision serves several useful functions:
- It defines the "gap" between where we are now and where we want to be.
- It creates a collective goal for all in the organization.
- It provides some basis for objectives and action plans.

A useful vision statement answers these questions:

- How will we be different, or better?
- What new roles or areas will we cover?
- What new measures of success will we have achieved?

Joel Barker's studies of vision researchers in the realms of nations, people and organizations suggest that visions need to be ...

- initiated by the organization's leaders.
- guided by the organization's values.
- shared with all those who must help make it a reality.
- clear and specific such that it can be visualized.
- supported by a "path" or strategies for fulfillment.

Objectives

Objectives are particular targets we aim for in order to achieve our vision. They are specific, measurable and time-framed targets that will accomplish results in critical areas of opportunity.

Objectives are most useful when they have some clear indicators or measures of achievement or key results.

> **Example:** To achieve user comfort, energy savings and complete integration of information and security in 3 "Smart Buildings" within 5 years. (Note the intention to be as specific as possible and numeric where possible.)

Strategy(ies)

"Strategy" defines the path we will follow to achieve our vision and our objectives; how we will close the "gap" between where we are now and where our vision calls for us to be.

> **Example:** We will gather the latest technology and combine it into one user-friendly system, beginning with Administrative Services and Information Technology and then invite academic areas to join in.

Strategies usually require a number of action plans ...

Action Plans

Action plans are the specific initiatives, programs, tasks or other activities we will undertake to accomplish our objectives and vision.

Effective Action Plans will identify:

- What and how
- When
- By whom

Some example action plans are shown in the following table (**Table 2**). They are related to the previous example objective and strategy.

Table 2: Action Plans

Action Plans	Target Date	Accountability of
1. Research and technology	7/95	Smith
2. Prepare program (sell all areas)	7/95	Jones
3. Finalize funding	1/96	White
4. Start first building	1/96	Vlack
5. Review with ASIT Division Management	every 6 months	Wang
6. Share with Academic Leaders	every 7 months	Khalidar
7. Involve Academic Leaders in Planning	6/96	Jensen

CHAPTER 6

A QUICK COURSE IN CHANGE AND CULTURE

Change, "culture" and "culture change" have been much discussed in the last decade. They've become common management terms and helpful words for all that. At its simplest "culture" means: **How we do things around here**. Culture represents how we behave, feel, decide and respond to events ... almost without thinking!

Culture is also the phenomenon that holds organizations stuck in their current modes.

More often now, managers and leaders puzzle over how to implement new plans, new procedures, new skills, new processes or even new systems such as TQM ... and how to have these desirable features or plans actually **become** part of the corporate culture.

What usually happens is that the corporate immune system (culture) rejects any change, even one that makes work easier, since change itself isn't comfortable for us.

Following (**Table 3**) are some helps and hindrances to changing corporate culture, presented in the form of a "Force Field." The force field is a helpful management problem definition format, first offered by Lewin.

Table 3: Helps and Hindrances for Change

GOAL: A company culture that responds to changes desired by management

Helping Forces (in rough priority order)	Hindering Forces (in rough priority order)
Strong, credible, repeated, forceful **statements** by respected managers and leaders, over time (a long time).	Lack of "constancy of purpose" in statements by managers and leaders, over time, seen as the "flavor of the month."
Changes in management practices: - individual and team goal-setting - performance-review - rewards & recognition - promotions & resource allocations These practices must drive toward the desired situation and be ... - well publicized - honestly followed	The "status quo" ... it's always more comfortable to face the known difficulty than the unknown. People wanting to **avoid** ... - more work - learning new skills - new habits to develop - new roles and relationships to understand

Helping Forces (in rough priority order)	Hindering Forces (in rough priority order)
Processes by which representative individuals or groups can be **involved** in or contribute to the planning and/or implementation work of the desired changes.	Providing no avenues or processes for input into or feedback about the changes being studied and/or implemented.
Not being diverted by distractions or even minor disasters, in our real priorities. This becomes a litmus test for our credibility.	Balky middle-managers who often feel caught in the middle. Their "survival approach" to life is a reaction to management's inconsistency.
Well-designed **training** and development that supports the desired changes, and is led by **managers**.	Expecting changes to happen quickly, painlessly or simply. Organizations are complex and change **is** difficult.
Rewarding well those in the vanguard of the changes. Making it costly for resistors and cynics to continue.	Not informing people well and often of the new needs and expectations.
Addressing **real** problems that arise with the changes, as people sort them out. This kind of follow-up can take 3 to 5 years!	Putting change management/leadership in "weak" hands; people who are unable or unwilling to make it happen.
Developing, educating and supporting change management teams of respected mid-level people who are ... - focused on major aspects of the change effort - well-resourced with time, tools and facilitation help - well-connected to top management - well-educated on change management concepts	Continuing with the usually terribly inefficient, time-wasting, nonproductive meetings that are typical of most organizations. **Not** having skills and concepts related to ... - process vs. content - facilitation and recording - flow-charting - teamwork

A Change Process Model

The following generic process (**Figure 7**) will often assist with any sort of desired change for an organization or any relatively autonomous unit of it. This process can be useful in planning change, or for diagnosing why a desired change may be stuck. It may be helpful as a **preliminary step**, **prior** to jumping into some specific process such as ...

- re-organizing
- strategic planning
- total quality management
- benchmarking
- re-engineering
- acquiring/merging
- downsizing

... and so on.

Figure 7: A Change Process

What unmet NEEDS are being felt or experienced?

What catalytic EVENTS are happening or may happen?

What are trends or projections telling you?

What is the organization's (or unit's) current MISSION?

What is the present situation?
- Strengths
- Opportunities
- Weaknesses
- Threats
- Trends and/or Projections

Identify the GAP between what IS and what's DESIRED. (What's missing?)

Figure 7: A Change Process ... Continued

What CHANGES* are or may be needed in:
- Services
- Products
- Programs
- Processes
- Staffing
- Structure
- Practices
- Systems
- Resources

---

*As you think about these changes, it will be quite important to remember these realities ...

- search for **facts**; avoid guessing.
- check out what **others** are doing.
- be creative; get out of the "box."
- people support what they help create.
- organizations are systems; a change in one part affects all other parts.
- unintended consequences will almost always happen.

Develop a PLAN to implement changes.

What **helping** forces must be mobilized? (Refer to Table 3.)

What **hindering** forces must be neutralized? (Refer to Table 3.)

Include a time schedule too.

Roll out the plan, including all the necessary ...
- background information (conte<u>xt</u>).
- how-to information (conte<u>nt</u>).
- changes to systems and phasing.
- orientation and training schedule.
- ongoing support and consultation.

Monitor progress and follow-up the plan.
- How's it going?
- Overlooked problems?
- Unintended consequences?

Make changes as needed or provide additional support required to reach intended outcomes.

Continue to monitor progress.

Other Thoughts

As to planning change, here are several important attitudes that may be helpful on occasion ...

- organizations are perfectly designed to get the results they currently get.

- if we plan to do what we always did, we'll get what we always got.

- no plan is perfect; plans must be monitored and then fine-tuned.

- 85% of the work of change comes after the planning, in implementation!

Finally, consultant Herb Shephard had some good, simple advice for planning changes ...

- know how people feel; begin with that in mind.

- start where people are the most ready.

- don't over-organize; keep it simple.

- build many fires; some will go out!

- reward and celebrate small successes!

CHAPTER 7

PLANNING FOR SUCCESSFUL STRATEGIES

Through many years of assisting boards, management teams or planning committees with their strategic planning work, we have searched for the elements of successful planning work. Here are some practical pointers and precautions that our clients and colleagues have found to be helpful.

1. Consider "strategic planning" as an **ongoing process**, year-round, rather than an event. Better still, consider it only a part of strategic thinking and management.

2. Study the planning work carefully using a **small steering committee**. One of its first tasks is to review the previous strategic plan and its success or failure. What was implemented (or not) and why?

3. Choose and utilize a planning group **representing the key components** of the organization: board, management, key committees, etc. Take care to keep the group small (eight persons or less) in order to be effective.

4. Recognize that different personalities will always bring different talents and perspectives to the work; these differences need to be **orchestrated and utilized** in order to be effective.

5. Developing reality-based data through **careful preparation** is essential. This may include market studies, image survey, peer review, employee ideas, financial performance studies, competitor benchmarking, client feedback, etc.

6. Recognize that energy and resources are limited and choose only those few **"key results areas"** that give the best return per unit of energy and per dollar. Address those few areas.

7. Go for a few **carefully chosen** strategic objectives that the team is very serious about. Write them in specific detail and support them with action steps.

8. The planning provides an excellent opportunity for management **team development** while doing the work of planning. Utilize it to the fullest and assess the stage of teamwork somewhere along the planning process. Enhanced teamwork will provide momentum for plan implementation.

9. Develop/assign/align an in-house **"champion" or leader** for each strategic objective, someone who will see it through to completion.

10. As part of the plan, create an effective means of **communicating** the appropriate parts of the plan to the various management and employee groups, including remote locations, subsidiaries, etc.

Now we'll explore each of these in a bit more detail.

Revisit the Practice of Strategic Planning

The best emerging management practice is to treat "strategic planning" as an ongoing (never finished) management process (not product), requiring clear strategic thinking (not "planning") by a board and/or management group/team. This approach is necessary due to ...

- easier/faster availability of needed information of all kinds.

- accelerating changes in the workplace, the economy and the world.

- rising expectations for quality of services and products.

Nevertheless, it still makes sense to do concentrated work on strategic thinking, review and planning periodically. How often depends on many factors, such as:

- The pace or rate of change in your markets.

- The pressure of your competitive situation.

- How difficult it is for planners to get together.

- Momentum from the last planning effort.

A major benefit of periodic and in-depth planning work is the opportunity to take a really good, fact-based look at how we're doing. This review of financial performance, productivity and work climate, management effectiveness, and client/service/product development will help to assure continuing viability of the organization.

Plan the Planning

A "steering committee" (senior manager and one or two others) is usually needed to plan the planning process, including selecting the planning group members.

Other important planning process questions to be considered by the steering committee are:

- Appropriate elements to be studied prior to the actual planning work (financial performance, peer review, market survey, etc.)

- Planning duration, dates, times, location and other logistics.

- The need for outside help in the form of a planning consultant, resource groups or special expertise.

- Invitations and needed background information for the planning group members.

Effective Planning Group

A planning group should meet several criteria to be successful at strategic thinking, review and planning. Group criteria that are important for most situations include:

- Representatives of all major functions.

- A group with reasonably good rapport.

- People who are respected by other employees.

- A mix of people-people, bottom-line people, visionaries and technically wise people.

- No more than eight people, though several additional individuals or groups may serve as resources to the planning group, for special assignments.

Often these criteria are available in an existing group such as board, management team, executive committee, partner group, directors or associates. If the board (or other governing body) isn't doing the planning, they may need to be involved in reviewing the proposed plan before it's adopted.

Developing Needed Data

A major difficulty facing many competently staffed planning groups is this: No one has identified the strategic issues facing the organization and no person or group has done much homework on the organization's situation or environment.

It's important to gather useful and needed information in the following areas:

- Financial performance trends and current status for various services, products, regions, client groups and functions.

- Market trends and current status, for all existing and potential services, regions, client groups and markets.

- Surveys of customers, clients, users and prospects, as to how the organization's work is perceived.

- Peer reviews or key employee reviews of operations, organization, morale, productivity, standards, quality and more.

This activity needs to be addressed by the steering committee in a timely way to avoid wasted effort or poorly focused planning.

One of the most useful and essential functions of strategic planning and problem-solving work is identifying and examining the assumptions we make about our services, our clients, our competitors, our economy, and so on.

Karl Albrecht, in his book *At America's Service* (published by Dow Jones Irwin, 1988) observes that the longer a firm (or agency) has been in existence, the more likely it is to ...

- take its clients for granted.

- be out of touch with their real needs.

- be uninformed about clients' perceptions.

Key Results Areas

Examples of key results areas that have often been addressed by planning groups are:

• Profitability.	• Information systems.
• Project management.	• Recruiting.
• Market changes.	• Growth and expansion.
• Organization structure.	• Training and development.
• Productivity.	• Teamwork.
• Quality improvement.	• Expanding services.
• Human resources.	• Mergers and acquisitions.
• Succession planning.	• Geographic expansion.
• Leadership needs.	• Ownership transition.

One way planning groups hurt their ability to implement is by overloading their plan with too many key results areas. Drucker notes that more than three key results areas is tantamount to having none.

So, it's essential to sift and prioritize the many possible key results areas of a plan, to whittle them down to a "precious few." Otherwise, the plan will look and feel overwhelming to those who must implement it.

Champions for Objectives

Generally speaking, a strategic plan addresses changes to the status quo, whether through improved effectiveness, new services or new clients, new owners or organizational roles, and so on.

Changes are quite naturally resisted by most of us, because they bring additional work and revised practices and priorities, and require new habits and/or relationships, inside and outside of the organization.

Inertia, old habits and hassle avoidance will block the progress of most strategic planning thrusts unless each such thrust (or objective) has an influential and high ranking **"champion"** or leader who will encourage and push all the people involved with it to commit the necessary time, work and resources.

As a practical matter, it's not usually a good idea to ask a person to champion more than two objectives and one is better yet.

It also helps to have each action step become the responsibility of a specific person or group who is directly responsible for its implementation.

Communicating the Plan

Plans that are restricted to the planning group or to senior management can do little to inspire or inform the organization's staff. When not kept informed of plans, the staff will often invent its own version (rumors) of the plan, based on scraps of (mis)information.

So, we usually recommend wide distribution of the plan. Most likely, all managers will need to see and support it. Several firms have found a "communication table" to be helpful. A sample is provided in **Table 4**.

When possible and cost-effective, the communication is best done face-to-face, whoever does it. People have the opportunity for questions, discussion and a much better understanding of the plan, so they are more likely to support it actively.

38

Table 4: Sample Communication Plan

Element (of plan) (1)	To whom (2)	By whom (3)	How (4)	When and where (5)
Mission	All staff	Chief executive officer	Meetings and video	January 1, 1995, at headquarters
Objectives	All staff	Chief executive officer	Meetings and video	January 1, 1995, at headquarters
Action steps	All managers	Their manager	Meetings and documents	Soon after January
Strengths and weaknesses	All managers	Their manager	Meetings and documents	Soon after January
Planning data and worksheets	Planning Group	Secretary to chief executive officer	Photocopies	ASAP

Suggested Elements of a Strategic Plan

Name and Time Frame of Plan.

Introduction and Background Information.

Mission (revised as necessary).

Vision Statement (if you want one).

Strengths, Weaknesses, Opportunities and Threats (brief and sanitized version).

Brief Summaries of:
- Client Feedback and
- Competitor Challenges.

Services Matrix (if you developed one).

Service Line Strategies (if appropriate).

Strategic Objectives.

Action Plans with Timetable and Accountabilities.

Program for Communication.

Schedule for Review of Progress.

Target Date for Renewing the Plan.

Participants Who Helped with the Plan.

Appendices, if any.

39

Detail Flow Chart for Strategic Thinking and Planning

> Small Steering Committee meets to design the process, time frame, planning, participants, location, etc.

- If an external consultant is to be used, include in the Steering Committee.
- Participants should represent all key functions and major geographic locations.

> Selected participants are advised of the purpose of the meeting, time, location and duration of meetings, preparation required with any read-aheads, etc.

- It is helpful to keep participant group as small as practicable.
- If external consultant is used, he/she needs to interview some or all participants before the working meeting.

> At the first meeting, participants look at recent past history, last plan results, strengths and weaknesses, client comments, competitor challenges, etc.

- Review results of **previous** plan.
- Review organization **Mission**.
- If desired, write a brief **Vision**.
- Assess **strengths and weaknesses** (internal).
- Scan environment for **opportunities and threats**.
- Review recent **client** comments/feedback.
- Check recent challenges from **competitors**.

> Based on that work, identify needed study tasks to be assigned to individuals or small groups to complete prior to the second meeting.

- Often study tasks relate to: new services, new opportunities, **specific problems** such as profitability, marketing, information systems, etc.
- Study groups or individuals do the requested investigations, **prepare conclusions** and, if appropriate, recommendations.

> At the second meeting, the Planning Team will hear, discuss and, if appropriate, amend the findings of individuals and study groups.

> Planners may find it useful to develop a 2 x 2 matrix of **Capabilities** (high to low) and **Attractiveness** (high to low) for their services and products and/or locations.

- This is often a helpful guide for developing **Strategic Objectives** or initiatives for: services, products, locations.

- **Capabilities** generally include staff expertise, depth and breadth; hardware and software, leadership, internal systems and special proprietary technologies.

- **Attractiveness** may include clients who are high quality, financially accountable and likely to be long term; also projects with positive image, relatively low risk and likely to be highly rewarding.

> Based on all previous work, planners identify the most important **strategic objectives** (or confirm them if some have **already** been identified).

- It is best to have relatively **few** objectives so that people can focus their energy on them.

- Look out at least 3 years; avoid a short-term (operational) focus.

> For each Strategic Objective, the planning team develops supporting Action Plans.

- List Action Plans (or initiatives).

- Identify who will be responsible for each.

- Set mileposts or time frames for each.

> The planning team also needs to design a means to communicate the plan to others, to review progress and renew the plan in the future.

- Develop a program for **communicating** the plan to management and staff at various levels, addressing their information needs and expected support.

- Set a schedule for **review** of progress and problems in implementation of the Strategic Plan, including amendments as necessary.
  - Quarterly reviews are recommended.
  - What gets reviewed gets **done!**

- Set a target for **re-doing** the plan from the ground up. Most firms and agencies find a 3-year time frame works well.

> To help assure implementation, the planners need to establish a process for business units to draw on the Strategic Plan to build their **annual operating plans**, which are different!

41

CHAPTER 8

GETTING THE PLAN IMPLEMENTED!

Sometimes it seems as if our organizations like strategic planning much more than strategic doing. Or as someone has said ... when all is said and done, more is said than done!

So ... **why** doesn't more of our strategic planning get **implemented** or **anchored** into reality? Many executives would love to know ... and so would we. Here's a list of six common reasons we've noted:

1. Data-based **study** of strategic issues isn't often done by small study teams or appropriate individuals.

    When plans aren't based on solid data, they may not be **worth** doing. So be sure your plans are data-based, not based on hot air!

2. By its very nature, good strategic planning is planning for **change**, for something beyond our "normal business momentum."

    And, as most of us have discovered, people generally tend to **resist** change because we are truly creatures of habit. We'll tackle this one later, in no. 6.

3. The very people who are the most effective, knowledgeable and appropriate for strategic planning, are usually the key leaders of the organization's geographic and/or functional areas.

    Wouldn't you know it ... they are **already** as busy as a one-armed organ grinder! So there must be some heavy-duty rewards or consequences to get their attention.

4. After the strategic issues have been given some careful data-based study and some strategic goals have been identified, there's one more crucial step that's often left undone.

    Those "goals" need to become true **objectives**, wherein they are **specific**, and ...

    *   measures or indicators are built in.
    *   responsible people or groups are identified.
    *   reasonable mileposts and time frames are noted.

5. Progress is seldom, if ever, reviewed or so it seems. Reviews are put off for lack of more "pressing matters."

However, what gets reviewed gets done. Progress on the action steps of the plan may not be measurable, but can usually be assessed in some subjective way. Having a schedule to review progress will help assure that there will indeed be **some** progress made!

- The most common approach is to use a quarterly meeting of the planning group to do a line-by-line review of: (1) progress (and some recognition for that); and (2) problems (and what can be done about them).

- Recognition of progress is important to help assure there will be more progress to celebrate later. "Recognition" simply means acknowledging the progress and recognizing those responsible for it. It should be simple and sincere.

- Problem solving is the way to keep the plan up-to-date with changes, unforeseen difficulties and unexpected opportunities. It doesn't require changing the "plan," but simple documentation is usually helpful, showing who, what, when, etc.

6.   Motivational elements are partly or totally lacking from most strategic plans. Most people do what gets reviewed or rewarded and **ignore** what seems to be of little consequence. This is particularly true when the work is out-of-the-ordinary.

Following are some **motivational** elements that seem to produce results:

- **recognition** for strategic results from one's boss or peers.

- the "broken record" technique, passionate **repetition** of our objectives.

- providing **team** recognition for strategic results worth celebrating, such as a new service, location, system, large customer, and so on.

- quarterly (or more frequent) **reviews** of strategic progress.

- tying strategic results to management **performance** reviews.

43

- encouraging business units, committees or task groups to be **creative** in action plans to achieve the objectives.

- **outside** board members, advisors or consultants who help remind us of our commitments and progress.

- **avoiding** confusion or loss of focus and what some have called management flavor-of-the-month.

Let's face it, brainstorming and free-wheeling discussion of opportunities (or even problems) is a lot more fun (and less demanding) than the grind-it-out work of implementation. Except for the most disciplined of people, **strategic motivation** is essential. To summarize then, here's what seems to help get strategic results:

- Recognition
- Repetition
- Team Recognition
- Reviews of Progress
- Performance Tie-in
- Encouraging Creativity
- Outside Observers
- Constancy of Purpose

What Is Success?

Professionals working on constructed facilities, designs, production programs, and the like are accustomed to seeing a high percentage of completion. Projects get finished, eventually.

Strategic planning, however, deals in a different realm with dicier assumptions, more ambiguous problems and less routine or familiar tasks, on top of an already heavy work load.

Given the foregoing constraints, 60% completion of a strategic plan within the original time targets is a high level of success! Even 50% completion is a respectable level.

So ... set realistic expectations ...

- review plan accomplishments periodically.
- be sure to applaud and recognize progress.
- incorporate new, unexpected opportunities.

CHAPTER 9

CRITICAL SUCCESS FACTORS FOR TQM

Today's business press has plenty to report on failed "Total Quality Management" efforts, after several years of great praise for TQM. Some reports suggest 3 of 4 efforts fail to meet expectations after large investments of time and money. Here's a sampler of recent headlines:

- "Quality Programs Show Shoddy Results" ... *The Wall Street Journal*

- "Totaled Quality Management" ... *The Washington Post*

- "The Cost of Quality" ... *Newsweek*

- "Ten Reasons Why TQM Doesn't Work" ... *Management Review*

Applications for the Baldrige Award have been dropping for several years. That, by the way, may be a positive sign for TQM, in that a number of award-winning firms have experienced financial and other problems soon after awards.

So, we must ask, and keep asking, what differentiates those firms that meet or exceed their expectations when implementing TQM: What are they doing or avoiding that leads to success?

From our clients in consulting engineering, construction, manufacturing, government and academia, we note the following "Critical Success Factors" ...

Discovery Period

- A key group of people have undertaken an extended period (several years) of **discovery** about TQM. During this time, members of the group explore

    ... the TQM literature.

    ... others' TQM experiences.

    ... visits/talks/books by TQM consultants.

    ... in-house experiences by their TQM "pioneers."

    ... Baldrige criteria and/or ISO registration requirements.

- This discovery period has enabled the group to make **enlightened** TQM decisions as to: if, how, where, with what help, and so on, based on a better understanding of TQM.

Senior Management

- Flowing from the discovery period, the key group has managed to inform, involve and get **senior management** in charge, if the "key group" wasn't senior management to begin with.

  The challenge here is to enable senior management to see that quality management is **their** issue, not one they can delegate, but one where they need to lead by example and work, not words. Senior management must visibly serve on the initial process improvement or corrective action teams!

Culture Change

- Often, as part of this process, senior management has found that "traditional" TQM wasn't quite right for them. They sensed a need for a system/process that **fit** the **organization's culture**, people and history. And often with its own special name, such as ...

  - Quality Plus.

  - Leadership by Client Satisfaction.

  - Achieving Total Customer Satisfaction.

  - Continuous Improvement.

- Though they might not have been able to articulate it, they sensed that TQM (or whatever they call it) required something of a **culture change** to succeed. They suspected it must impact their ...

  - basic work processes.

  - management's time.

  - organization roles.

  - rewards and recognition.

Steering Team

- Successful organizations formed a senior level **Steering Committee** (or Team) to continue to learn but also to carefully guide the TQM process across the organization. Some specific tasks include:

  - Selecting sites for implementation.

  - Orienting key staff on TQM.

  - Getting outside help as needed.

  - Helping develop the training required.

46

Scope of TQM

- They found that TQM isn't only about "quality" but it's also about "management." Stated mathematically ...

  TQM = management of **quality**,

  and TQM $\equiv$ quality of **management**.

  TQM is about improving customer satisfaction through continuous improvement of everything that matters to customers.

Spartan Approach

- Many organizations are experiencing tight budgets (public sector), tight markets (private sector) and an uncertain future (everybody). And as a result, successful TQM organizations approached implementation efforts on an adequate but **Spartan** budget; leveraging every dollar and hour spent.

ISO 9000 Isn't TQM

- Organizations thinking about TQM learned that ISO 9000 is not about quality management; it concerns **Standards**. ISO 9000 certifies only that we do what we say we do ... however good or poor that may be.

  We recommend that TQM be well-implemented before tackling ISO 9000 certification in most cases. Also, at this time ISO certification is of questionable value for the high cost unless your customers are requiring certification.

Training Where Needed

- Once they began to grasp the essence and potential of TQM, successful organizations didn't begin a broadside of "education" or training all employees. They knew their people expected to be significantly involved after any training!

  Training was provided **just in time** for those specific groups, areas, departments (or whatever) who were then actively involved in TQM projects and processes.

Early Efforts

- Early TQM improvement efforts focused on very **significant** and specific needs for organization improvement, directed at some combination of ...

  - assessing/improving client satisfaction.

  - improving a key process.

- tackling a chronic problem area.

- improving productivity and/or profitability.

- In some organizations, early efforts were focused too much on internal improvements that had little, if any, impact on customer satisfaction. They overlooked the point that quality and value are (to a large degree) defined by their customers!

    Zenger-Miller said it well in their book *Leading Teams: Mastering the New Role* (published by Business One Irwin, 1993): "The list is now expanding to 'better, faster, cheaper' -- and newer!"

Customer Focus

- In a similar vein, TQM has produced little of value for the investment if it's overly focused on reductions in defects or errors. Minimum standards don't define quality. **Customers** do. And they want features that provide more and better service. They expect reliability as a given.

- Keki Bhote notes in *Next Operation as Customer (NOAC)* (published by the American Management Association, 1991) ... Customer enthusiasm depends not only on quality, timeliness and cost, but it also depends upon dependability, cooperation and communication!

Few but Good

- Effective groups recognized it's **not** how many TQM teams are started, but how **successful** the early teams were, because they were well-supported.

    From these early successful experiences, TQM was transplanted across the organization, because other people wanted it in their areas. It spread by **contagion** rather than by management edict.

TQM Staffing

- Problems with TQM occurred when many new "TQM" positions were added. TQM must be the job of line management from top to bottom. It fails if delegated. Yet, a **few** skilled support staff may be needed to help with ...

- training and development.

- facilitating improvement teams.

- cross-pollinating TQM across the organization.

Fact-Based Management

- Successful TQM brought "fact-based management" to organizations in ways seldom experienced. What passes for "problem solving" in most organizations is really "tampering" in a TQM sense or "hip-shooting" in the vernacular.

  This doesn't mean that all TQM efforts become exercises in statistics, but rather that TQM requires an appreciation for **facts**.

Customer Feedback

- Similarly, the organizations that made TQM **work** for them became well acquainted with ...

  - customer feedback on features they care about,

  - measures of quality that lead to those features,

  - benchmarking good competitors on measures,

  ... and they made use of these criteria and data to **know** where to target improvement work next!

Continuous Improvement

- Firms that have found TQM useful and helpful have also found plenty of help in the ideas and experiences of their clients/customers, suppliers/vendors, respected competitors and TQM consultants.

  They are in a **continuous** and deliberate mode of discovery to continuously improve their understanding and applications of TQM. Here are a few samples:

  - Xerox was 5 years into their TQM effort when they studied their situation and began again. Their success led to their market resurgence in the U.S.

  - Walker Consultants experienced TQM success based on the principles of Phil Crosby. However, now they see a need to examine Deming's perspectives for what they may offer.

  - University of Cincinnati Facilities Management, chalking up major savings while increasing customer satisfaction, is starting to look for ways to increase inter-departmental teamwork.

Other Thoughts

Consultant Joe Jablonski of Albuquerque, New Mexico, believes that TQM is **better** than free; it pays dividends after the initial investment!

Consultant Bill Hayden of Jacksonville, Florida, offers the following observations about TQM to both skeptics and fanatics:

- It's not going away.
- TQM can't be delegated.
- Every day more clients demand it.
- Success isn't measured by the number of teams you start.
- The measure of leadership is not found in their words.
- The one who dies with the most charts does not win.

I would add that, generally speaking, the significant value organizations get from TQM is:

- Directly related to the time key people take to study it **before** the plunge.
- Directly related to the **number** of sources of information and others' experiences they explore first.
- Directly related to **senior** management involvement in their early TQM efforts.
- Directly related to focusing on processes or areas needing **major** improvement.
- Inversely proportional to the amount of **new** money spent on it.
- Inversely proportional to the number of people who "get training."
- Inversely proportional to the number of new people hired to help with Quality.

Getting Good Help

We've made several recommendations to our clients for TQM **consultants** that we've later come to regret. Clients weren't happy with them. These have been well-known folks, but they weren't successful in our referrals.

However we have found several very helpful reference **books** to guide you through your TQM work, and clients **have** been happy with them!

- **All the books** by Phil Crosby and Edwards Deming are well worth reading by **someone** on your "discovery" team. They're available in most libraries and some bookstores.

- *Collective Excellence: Building Effective Teams* by Mel Hensey, published by the American Society of Civil Engineers, 345 East 47th Street, New York, New York 10017-2398, 1992.

- *Implementing TQM;* Revised Second Edition, by Joseph Jablonski, published by Technical Management Consortium, Inc., Albuquerque, New Mexico, 1994.

- *Making Quality Work* by Labovitz, Chang and Rosansky, published by Harper Business Division of Harper Collins Publishers, New York, 1993.

- *Quality by Design*, a quality management newsletter for Architects, Engineers and Constructors, by William M. Hayden, Jr. Consultants, Inc., Jacksonville, Florida.

- *The Team Handbook* by Peter R. Scholtes and other contributors, published by Joiner Associates, Inc., 3800 Regent Street, Madison, Wisconsin, 1990.

These books cover different aspects of TQM and probably all of them belong in any comprehensive library of quality management.

CHAPTER 10

BENCHMARKING ... EASY AND NECESSARY

If anyone should understand **"benchmarks"** or **"benchmarking"** it must surely be engineers, and particularly civil engineers! This historically civil and surveying term has been given new life in the context of continuous excellence!

This new usage of the term benchmarking occurs in a variety of ways. It has evolved a lot from its early use by Xerox, Motorola, GE, Ford and other TQM pioneers. No longer is it focused primarily on measures and statistics.

In the steadily increasing scope of benchmarking, we note at least three helpful directions:

- **Benchmarks:** Indicators or **measures** useful as guides to improving practices, processes, functions or performance.

- **Benchmarking:** A continuous **search** for the "best" practices, processes or functions, using a rigorous approach.

- **Informal Benchmarking:** A less rigorous approach to learning from others about **anything** that will improve operations, quality, customer satisfaction, value (cost) or time.

Benchmarking Steps

C.E. Bogen and M.J. English in *Benchmarking for Best Practices* (published by McGraw-Hill, Inc., 1994) have a very useful 5 step process for what I call "rigorous benchmarking." It is: Launch, Organize, Reach out, Assimilate and Act.

The only step that perhaps needs amplification is **Launch**; the authors suggest it's very important to study and decide what **key areas** the benchmarking organization wants to benchmark.

For example, a firm having less than a successful approach to Project Management might well focus benchmarking efforts on that narrow but crucial aspect of work.

While assisting our clients with benchmarking, we've found that other consulting/design firms have been **extraordinarily** helpful in providing information on their internal processes and practices like these:

- Project management.
- Strategic planning.
- Total Quality Management.
- Project cost status reporting.

- Incentive compensation.
- Marketing and sales.
- Peer reviews.

Making It Work

For manufacturing or industrial firms, or even for service organizations with a lot of repetitive work (such as a facility management group), it seems that **"rigorous** benchmarking" makes a lot of sense.

However, for organizations such as constructors, consulting engineers, environmental consultants and public agencies that deal with relatively large and unique projects, **informal** benchmarking provides more value, faster, with less crapola.

What we're really after with **informal** benchmarking is simply ...

Learning Quickly from Others

The goal is to take what others are willing to share, and then **adapt** and **adopt** it to our own use if and as appropriate.

This also requires some innovation in most cases, and some modesty and humility in almost all cases. Bogen and English refer to such firms or agencies as FLOs ... "fast learning organizations."

They point out that we need to learn to **learn easily** from others, as well as from our own creativity and mistakes. I suspect that this ability is rapidly becoming a **survival skill**. The Japanese have been modest masters of it, teaching the rest of the world how it pays off.

Internal Benchmarking

Over the years of assisting our clients with strategic planning and related kinds of work, we've encouraged them to do some data gathering to give their goals and plans a more solid basis.

When they've been reluctant to contact competitors for data (or even if they weren't reluctant) we've helped them see they have a lot of useful data on their best competitors already in very handy forms:

- Their recent experienced hires.
- Their temporary employees.
- Their sub-consultants and suppliers.
- Their clients' knowledge of competitors.
- Their professional associations.

And, it's worth repeating that so-called competitors in other firms and agencies are **incredibly** helpful!   And they are very willing to share useful information on their practices, processes and approaches, as well as their **failures and problem areas**.

External Benchmarking

With the increasing number of newsletters, journals and conferences serving most any sector of the services industry, it's quite easy to get helpful information on:

- What other, similar firms are doing.

- What the average of firms in your sector are doing.

For example, Patricia Hecker, a VP of Operations for Olsson Associates, Consulting Engineers (Lincoln, Nebraska) gave a talk at the ASCE Engineering Management Division Conference in Chicago, April of 1995.   She provided **detailed "Lessons Learned"** in how Olsson manages and develops their people!

What's Important?

The term **benchmarking** may conjure up visions of sophisticated, complex procedures. It's important to stay focused on the true value inherent in what we've called "benchmarking":

- **Our clients and customers** frequently "benchmark" us against our competitors.

- **More will be learned and faster** by benchmarking than improvements developed in-house.

- **So called "best practices"** won't stay best for long; so aim for **continuous** excellence!

CHAPTER 11

BUSINESS PROCESS RE-ENGINEERING

Business Process Re-engineering (and re-inventing) is very much akin to Total Quality Management (TQM) in its goals. However, these approaches differ in some important ways:

- TQM requires that we flow-chart all key processes, gather and analyze data on troublesome aspects and **improve** them continually over time.

- Re-engineering begins with customer needs and feedback, then designs the key process(es) from **scratch**, laying aside all existing constraints and assumptions.

While TQM aims generally at incremental and continuous improvements to business processes, Re-engineering aims for **breakthrough** redesign and radical change.

Early thoughts on business process "Re-engineering" were advanced by Michael Hammer in his July-August 1990 *Harvard Business Review* article, which triggered a variety of approaches.

What is common to the various approaches being tried and used is this:

Senior executives try to set aside their current assumptions about a particular business process, view it from a customer or client perspective, and re-invent it without being bound by existing constraints, traditions, etc.

Success Factors

Tim Davis, writing in July-August 1993 *Planning Review*, identifies six success factors from speakers at a Manufacturing Institute conference in January 1993. His six success factors are hardly surprising, but are worth noting here:

1. External forces are driving for changes in ways that cannot be ignored.

2. Senior management must support the effort with leadership, funds and incentives.

3. Re-engineering should begin with customer/client needs, wants and concerns.

4. Most efforts will require considerable consulting assistance from both outside and inside the organization.

5. Interdisciplinary teams of key managers from all areas of the affected process must be involved (and well led).

6. Expect changes in human resource practices and information systems, to support the new process(es).

These same factors, in my view, are required for successful implementation of TQM. The lack of factors like these, plus others, has led to the high percentage of "failures" in TQM efforts.

Executives must ask: "If I were starting this company (agency) today, given what I (we) know and given current (emerging) technology, what would it look like?" This key question is posed by Michael Hammer and James Champy in *Re-engineering the Corporation* (published by Harper Business, 1993).

It's necessary to set aside **all** assumptions and presuppositions, and take **nothing** for granted. Our experience suggests this is easier said than done, but a carefully chosen team and team leader can make it happen.

Goals for re-engineering include ... moving from "departments" to seamless work processes, simplifying processes wherever possible, elimination of layers and inspection, focusing on teams more than roles or task specialization.

More Factors!

To Tim Davis' list of Re-engineering success factors, we would have to add the following:

7. Well-chosen team and team leader, highly respected by all employees, and of course supported by top management.

8. Elapsed time, and **lots** of it, to delve into what others have done and various approaches, before beginning the actual work.

9. Enough freed-up time from other regular responsibilities, so the team and leader **can** do their work.

10. Help at team building and skill building with group process tools. This will need to be the **most** effective team in the organization!

11. Appropriate management **leverage** applied wherever needed in the organization, for the team to get what it needs.

12. As the business process moves from Re-engineering to Re-construction, recognize that people will need about **twice** as much time, education, coaching, involvement and communication as seems reasonable!

Typical Benefits

Many of the benefits are obvious, others are less so. Following are some benefits reported by university administrators, computer manufacturers, consulting engineers and public service organizations:

- Elimination of some functions altogether (though not necessarily the elimination of people).

- Elimination or reduction of narrow task specialties, job titles, etc., in favor of more generalists.

- Reduction of cross-overs, hand-offs and sign-offs between internal departments, functions or groups.

- Reductions in internal documentation and checking, within functions and within the whole organization.

- Enhanced internal communication, which, **not** coincidentally, is one of the most frequent customer complaints about service organizations of all kinds!

- Ditto all the above with regard to suppliers. Suppliers may become more integral with the process(es).

Observations

Generally, **Re-engineering** may be easier in the **planning** phase, while **Process Improvement** may be easier to **implement**.

As to which approach to use, the only guidelines we can suggest are these:

- Key business processes should **always** have champions and process improvement teams.

- When Key business processes seem to be unsalvagable, Re-engineering them may be more cost effective in the long run.

- Don't waste time Re-engineering marginal processes — those that **aren't** crucial to your customer service and success.

- The developers of Re-engineering note that many so-called Re-engineering projects aren't that at all; in fact they are improvements.

Re-engineering has **not** been more successful than TQM in terms of its successes and failures. **George Washington** may have recognized this in his second inaugural address when he said, "One of the difficulties in bringing about change in an organization is that you must do so through persons who have been most successful in that organization, no matter how faulty [it] is."

CHAPTER 12

STARTING NEW OFFICES, SERVICES OR BUSINESS UNITS

Most of our clients have had considerable experience at opening new offices, services or business units in a period of growth and expansion.

Most of them have also had the (sad) experience of closing down several ... after spending talent and treasure propping them up.

Several firms have really studied their unsuccessful experiences to identify the "critical success factors" that spell the difference between hits and misses.

General Success Factors

Following are some of the factors that seem to apply regardless of whether you're starting a new office **or** a new business unit:

- Making a careful study of the actual business climate.

- Teaming with a large local client, a "partner" firm or another division.

- Providing the needed support in dollars, staff, marketing assistance, help with production capacity, and such.

- Putting a very talented start-up marketer/leader/doer "in charge."

Start-up Team Leader

This may actually be the most important factor when all is said and done. The reason so few start-up team leaders really make it work is that they must be so **multi**-talented.

Most managers have significant strengths but also weaknesses. The key to success with a start-up manager is making sure he/she has the particular strengths needed for the start-up situation. Our clients tell us that **not** having these particular strengths almost always leads to trouble:

- Knowledge of the firm (which may rule out most new hires).

- Possessing the credentials (experience, registration, credibility) required for the situation.

- Appreciation of local customs, politics, buying patterns, key people to link with, and so on.

- Ability to hire and lead good people who can grow into more responsibility.

- Knowledge of the financial fundamentals: pricing, controlling expenses and collections.

- Ability to quickly build relationships and sell the firm to clients.

- Ability to sniff out projects or services where the firm can compete.

- Great energy and willingness to put in a huge amount of "sweat equity."

While all of these are necessary to success ... and well proven by failures, the last item is the hardest to fulfill. In some start-up situations, it requires motivation almost to the level of obsession.

It's little wonder that *Professional Services Management Journal* suggested that your next CEO should be a former branch office manager. The April 1993 issue of PSMJ notes that these managers must be mini CEO's running their own little firm. (And, in most cases, without much help.)

Market Research

"Research," or just plain digging out the data, is essential to knowing what your opportunity is ... or isn't.

Shortening this process to save time or money could likely cost a **lot** more to recover later or punt in a badly chosen situation.

Several clients have found the best approach for this situation assessment is to commit several people experienced in marketing, sales and operations. They need to visit and study for whatever time it takes to size up ...

- the business climate and trend.

- competitors and how they're doing.

- clients' needs and buying processes.

As they visit, meet people and gather perceptions, several clients have found the following sources will provide helpful information ...

- large developers.

- commercial realtors.

- economic development councils.

- managers of local industries.

- chambers of commerce.

- bankers and business attorneys.

- possible partners, subs or primes.

- local colleges or universities.
- managers of office parks and buildings.
- governmental unit managers.

Other Essentials

A "big brother" office that is hopefully close, but more than that, willing to help in real ways, such as marketing and sales help, project production, clerical help and more ... is of great value.

If the start-up is a new **service**, it's often important to have (or find) someone who is well known and respected in that field; someone who can quickly build credibility with potential clients.

A frequent pitfall for new services is that no one on the board of directors or the management committee really understands it as well as they understand existing services. This often results in one of two problems:

- Lack of senior management review and guidance ... and consequent lack of performance.
- Amateurish nit-picking about costs, because that's the easiest part to review critically.

Consider the start-up an investment, not a cost. Expect it to take 2 to 4 years to develop, years in which you may need to make further financial commitments.

However, in 2 to 4 years, expect the start-up to be in the black and paying a return on your investment. If it isn't, make a careful study and be prepared to make a significant change, such as ...

- assignment of additional corporate support.
- replacement of key on-site management.
- cutback, shutdown or redirection.
- merge with another office.
- sale to another firm.

With thanks and a tip of the hat to ...

Bissell and Karn
Dames and Moore
Lockwood, Jones and Beals
Soil and Material Engineers
Terracon Consultants
Woolpert Consultants
... among others

CHAPTER 13

"TEAMS" AND ORGANIZATIONAL IMPROVEMENT

Teams and organizational improvement ... go together like the proverbial ham and eggs. That's so, whether talking about Total Client Service, TQM, Re-engineering, Employee Empowerment or the next iteration.

Here's why: A major part of any improvement effort must focus on total systems or processes. No individual or functional unit can get its arms around a total system or process. It takes a team!

In the typical professional services firm, teams are much talked about. Sometimes groups actually do perform as TEAMS! As described in *Collective Excellence* (published by ASCE, 1992), "teams" have certain operating characteristics that separate them from groups.

Following are the kinds of teams (or groups) that are often useful and necessary:

- **Strategic Planning Team:** This may be a task group or on-going group or even an existing group, such as the Board of Directors.

- **Quality Steering Team:** The **top "steering committee"** for TQM, usually led by the senior executives.

- **Quality Operations Team:** TQM management team for a particular **region** or **division** of the firm.

- **Training and Development Team:** A team focused on **culture change** through education, for the firm or a large unit.

- **Benchmarking Teams:** Teams, often spread over the geography of the firm, which continuously network with other firms as well as clients, to assess **"how we're doing"** on the key indicators of quality and client service.

- **Process Improvement Teams:** Teams focused on continually improving **"processes"** of particular importance to quality and client service. Such teams usually cut across several or all functions (marketing, project management, design, finance, human resources, etc.). Typical examples ...
  - project selection/proposal/contracting process.
  - project implementation/delivery process.

- **Corrective Action or Breakthrough Teams:** Short-term teams charged with addressing a nasty **systems** problem affecting **multiple** projects.

- **Strategic Alliances:** Long-term teams with a senior-level perspective and aim of developing **strategic alliances** with clients or suppliers or partner firms (JV's or subs) to further quality, client service, teamwork and mutual support.

- **Project Partnerships:** Short-term teams formed among client, engineer and/or contractor for a single project to increase teamwork, reduce claims, etc. Often done for public works projects where law forbids strategic alliances.

- **Re-engineering Teams:** Multi-functional teams charged with looking at the whole organization or a significant chunk of it, to re-think it and re-invent it.

While few firms seem to have all these types of teams, the firms farther along have many of these types of teams (though they probably use different terminology to describe them).

Team Development

The effectiveness of these kinds of teams, as in all teams, will depend upon team **development**. Teams may or may not develop to an effective level (Stage 3 or 4, with reference to Figure 5 in *Collective Excellence*, mentioned earlier).

Team development cannot be taken for granted; intention and effort is necessary. This is particularly so for team members from different parts of the organization.

Figure 8, Team Flow Chart (following), offers several suggestions for helping teams develop as they do their regular work. Other suggestions are available in *Collective Excellence*.

Too many tasky team leaders forget about most needs and activities except for the bottom box **(tasks)**. They either fail to realize the other needs (boxes) are necessary ... or they wait until the team is hurting before they act.

```
┌─────────────────────────┐
│   Leader who listens and │
│   helps the group with   │
│   both task and process  │
└─────────────────────────┘

┌──────────────────────┐              ┌──────────────────────┐
│ Using any of these team│             │ Simple structure and │
│ metrics, ask group to  │             │ time and place to get │
│ assess itself often ...│             │ even better acquainted as│
│                        │             │ people                │
│ - Characteristics of   │             └──────────────────────┘
│   effective teams      │   Resources
│                        │    and
│ - Team stages chart    │   Activities
│                        │      to        ┌──────────────────────┐
│ - Effective team       │   Develop      │ Develop/clarify/discuss│
│   members              │    Teams       │ together ...          │
└──────────────────────┘                 │                       │
                                          │ - Mission    - Norms, │
┌──────────────────────┐                 │ - Goals       Values  │
│ Plan and do something │                 │ - Roles       or      │
│ social and fun together│                │ - Procedures  Ground  │
│ from time to time     │                 │               rules   │
└──────────────────────┘                 └──────────────────────┘

        ┌──────────────────────┐
        │ Tackle significant team│
        │ tasks together from time│
        │ to time               │
        └──────────────────────┘
```

This flow chart is **multi**-directional; that is, the arrows may go clockwise, counterclockwise, or from any box to any other box. What's important is that each "activity" occur with some frequency! The chart was first developed (by Mel) at the Greiner Engineering Qplus Workshop for Quality Leaders in August 1993.

Figure 8: Team Development Flow Chart

Deborah Harrington-Mackin's research on teams in all walks of life and work was helpful in determining a common feature of effective teams: They have "rules," norms or guidelines for how they'll operate and work together. **Figure 9** (following) shows one way to assure that your team has what it may need.

Team Name? _____

Team Purpose? _____

_____

Expected Results? _____

_____

_____

Membership? _____

_____

_____

Key Individual Roles on the Team?

- Leader _____
- Recorder _____   May Rotate? _____
- Facilitator _____

Team Goals, Values, Rules or Expectations Regarding Trust, Communication, Openness, Conflict, Participation, and such? _____

_____

_____

_____

Regular Meeting Time and Place? _____

Typical Agenda Format? _____

_____

_____

Handle "Leftovers" By? _____

_____

_____

Regular Visual Aids? _____

_____

_____

Orient New Members By? _____

_____

_____

Basis of Team Review for Self-improvement? _____

_____

Developed by Hensey Associates
based on our Partnering experiences and inspired by
Deborah Harrington-Mackin's *The Team Building Tool Kit*

Figure 9: Essentials for Forming (or Re-forming) a Team

Inter-Team Collaboration

In a climate and culture for Continuous Improvement, teams will more often need to work well together, aiming for the seamless organization their clients expect. **Table 5** shows three stages of such inter-team work, which can be used in several ways.

Table 5: Inter-Team Collaboration
Interdependent Teams and Groups May Work Together Well or Poorly

Stage A Non-Functioning	Stage B Functioning	Stage C Inter-Team Work
Groups tend to view one another with mistrust and suspicion.	Groups tend to view one another as essential, but have many complaints about others' performance.	Groups tend to view one another as essential and treat one another with respect, even when problems occur.
Exchange of objective, unbiased information between groups is minimal.	Necessary information is exchanged in a business-like way; no more, no less.	Necessary information is exchanged promptly, both formally and informally; the objective is to help.
Information available in one group about the other group is often ... • biased. • inaccurate. • full of assumptions. • the worst possible interpretation.	Information available in one group about the other group is often factual, but still includes some ... • untested assumptions. • overblown complaints.	Information available in one group about the other is usually ... • factual. • fair. • current. • objective.
Any group member seen as defending or supporting the other group is viewed as a fool at best, traitor at worst.	There are members within both groups who have good relationships, and who stand up for the **other** group.	Most members of both groups have good relationships; those who do not are encouraged to work it out.

Stage A Non-Functioning	Stage B Functioning	Stage C Inter-Team Work
Conflicts grow over time, creating even more of the above difficulties, often resulting in **feud** behavior.	Conflicts flare up, usually due to real problems, and are generally handled well by a few key people who are skilled at it.	Conflicts between groups are seen as natural and inevitable. Processes exist and are used by most members to resolve conflicts quickly in a win/win mode if at all possible.
Work processes that cut across groups become more redundant and complex as the groups ... • defend turf. • build silos. • create CYA safeguards.	Cross-cutting work processes are a source of irritation, but generally work satisfactorily. There is often good teamwork by pairs of people who work at the groups' interfaces, sometimes better than their managers.	Cross-cutting work processes are handled with care and attention; "down-stream" colleagues are treated as "internal customers." These work processes are continuously improved and simplified, with roles shifting as necessary.

Perhaps the most useful thing to be done with this table is to:

- Ask teams to assess their stage of inter-team work.
- Ask them what could improve it, if that seems desirable.
- Discuss, sort, choose and implement several of these possible improvements.

CHAPTER 14

PARTNERING: MUCH ADO ABOUT SOMETHING!

Having looked at the importance of **teams** to organizational improvement, we really ought to address **Partnering**, a significant contribution to the world of work in most any field.

Recently a faculty member and client looked puzzled at a news brief on Partnering. "What's 'Partnering?'" he asked. As I thought about his question, these are the responses that sprang to mind as definitions of "Partnering":

- An alternative to disputes, claims and dispute resolution.

- An important part of Total Quality Management (TQM).

- Back to the way we used to do business, with openness and trust.

- Team building between project contributors who may sometimes be adversaries.

- A new way of doing design and/or construction projects, together as one team.

- "A concept that creates a win/win attitude among all the team players" ... *A Concept for Success* [Associated General Contractors (AGC)].

- "When we choose to live by the spirit, rather than the letter of the law" ... *Engineering News Record* (ENR) [published by McGraw-Hill], February 11, 1991.

- "Partnering is a long-term commitment between two or more organizations for the purpose of achieving specific business objectives by maximizing the effectiveness of each participant's resources" ... Partnering Task Force of the Construction Industry Institute (CII), July 1991.

- "By taking steps before construction begins to change the adversarial mindset, to recognize common interests and to establish an atmosphere of trust and candor in communication, Partnering helps develop a cooperative management team" ... **Pamphlet 4 of** *Alternative Dispute Resolution Services* (U.S. Army Corps of Engineers, December 1991).

Parts of Partnering

Partnering is all this and more. It's a **deliberate, planned team approach** to a project at any stage. These are some of the important steps along the way:

- **Realization** that there is an alternative to disputes, claims, legal actions, etc.

- **Desire** to work together in more of a team approach, a "Partnership" in spirit, though not in a legal sense.

- **Invitation** by one party to "Partner" with the others, with the suggestion that they commit to the up-front effort to make it work.

- **Working** through a Partnering kick-off meeting of all (then known) parties to the project, which then sets the stage for Partnering through the rest of the project.

- **Establishing** a Partnering "Charter" as part of the meeting, to guide the Partnership through the rest of the project, samples of which are given in the excellent Corps and AGC booklets.

- **Follow-through** on the Charter; meeting, working, deciding and problem solving in the spirit and manner developed at the kick-off meeting.

Kick-off Meeting

Our consulting work has shown us that teams of **any** kind may go through four stages, called ...

Forming   Storming   Norming   Performing

(after Tuckman) ... and that getting through the first two stages requires **face to face** work by the team. After that, team members can more easily do effective work even while geographically separated from one another.

Kick-off meetings should be focused on tasks the team will need to have **agreement** on and/or be able to fall back on in the months and years ahead:

- Mission of the Partnership.
- Objectives for communication and performance.
- Types of working meetings.
- Typical project problems to be handled.
- Conflict/Problem Resolution Process.

A few exercises that bring **people** together as people may also be valuable. However, clients tell us they prefer not to spend major time on "games" and they like activities that help them get to know one another better as **individuals**.

Proposed Ground Rules for Partnering Meetings

Kick-off meetings and other Partnering meetings seem to go much better if the Partnership agrees to some ground rules. These are typical and could serve most any group:

1. **Don't** interrupt whomever is talking. Hold your questions, disagreements, etc., on a note pad for later.

2. **Listen** well enough to be able to paraphrase others, even when you disagree with them.

3. **Avoid** side conversations during the meetings, they disrupt the work and cause us to lose important points.

4. **Stay** focused on the topic at hand. If you need to tackle another issue, ask the group to change topics.

5. **Expect** disagreement. Don't personalize it. **Attack problems**, not people.

6. **When brainstorming**, do not criticize others' ideas. Asking for elaboration or clarification is OK. If you dislike an idea, suggest a better one!

7. Unless making a report, hold your comments to two minutes. That's plenty unless you are ...

   - repeating.
   - filibustering.
   - selling.
   - confused.

8. Be willing to compromise and look for win/win solutions for the group.

Results of Partnering

Experience suggests that owners, designers and constructors of facilities will set **tougher** goals **together** than they could ever gain agreement on outside the realm of Partnering. And, they are goals that require commitment and contribution by **all** parties.

Generally speaking, there are more claims and hassles, more opportunities for finger-pointing, blame-placing and ass-covering in the public sector than the private. In all cases though, these are the benefits that participants report:

- Less suspicion and mistrust of others.
- Faster turn-around on reviews and approvals.
- Faster decisions on field problems and contingencies.
- Fewer claims, settled faster and less contentiously.
- Shorter schedules with fewer overruns/delays.
- Closer adherence to budgets and estimates.
- Higher quality at completion/occupancy.
- Less hassle for public and neighbors.
- Completion without litigation.
- Few accidents or injuries.

How to Kill Partnering

There is a natural tendency to want to make Partnering automatic, mandatory and routine. Examples of that are: shortening the kick-off meeting, lack of senior level participation, always doing the charter in a particular way, coercing parties into the partnership, automating the agenda, and so on. Such things will kill the essential deep-level communication and personal commitment that have made Partnering so successful.

Further Information

- Thomas R. Warne has written an excellent reference: *Partnering for Success* (published by ASCE, 1994).
- Jim Brown's feature article **"Partnering to Save Troubled Projects"** (published in ASCE's *Journal of Management in Engineering*, May/June 1994) is full of good ideas.
- Both the U.S. Army Corps of Engineers and the Associated General Contractors (AGC) have written excellent guides to Partnering.

CHAPTER 15

COMMUNICATION AND EXCELLENCE

So much has been spoken and written about communication ... dare we say more? Yet, communication is so necessary to achieving organizational excellence that a few things really **do** need to be said.

First, there are four major **barriers** to effective communication in all kinds of organizations that we need to watch out for. These barriers can literally block any organizational assessment, improvement or development if they aren't understood and dealt with.

1. **Group Communication (The Undiscussable)**

    Chris Argyris gives a unique view in *Overcoming Organizational Defenses* (published by Prentice-Hall, 1990) and a simple message about organizational effectiveness:

    > The **biggest** problem in most organizations today is the operative norm that most of our serious problems are undiscussable (in official work meetings) and the fact that they are undiscussable is also undiscussable.

2. **One to One Communication (Triangulation)**

    Freidman, writing in *Generation to Generation* (published by Guilford Press, 1985), adds an interesting twist ... he notes that organizations of all kinds have this chronic problem:

    > **"Triangle** communication" is the norm. That is: Ralph talks to Mary about his problems with Tom, but seldom if ever directly to Tom. And Tom talks to Mary about his problems with Ralph ... and so on and so forth.

3. **Boss/Subordinate Communication (No Feedback)**

    Mardy Grothe and Peter Wylie in *Problem Bosses* (published by Facts on File, 1987) believe that every boss in one way or another is a problem to his or her employees, though most bosses don't think they are.

Part of this problem is that most bosses are insulated from feedback from their staff on how they're doing, what people need from them and so on. And because no one tells them, they figure they must be doing pretty well.

4.   Intentions vs. Effects (Distortion)

Over the years and still today, I'm often mystified that what I'd intended to communicate came across to others **very** differently than I'd intended!

Figure 10 shows this angle of distortion between intentions and effects. Here are some of the causes of this distortion:

- My choice of words and phrases.
- My non-verbal communication.
- Inattentive listening by the other person(s).
- Cultural and/or language differences.
- Either person being distracted or upset.

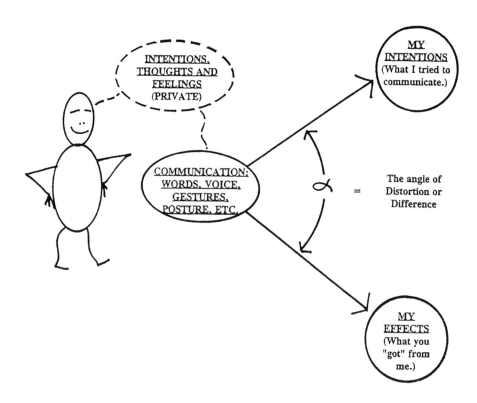

Figure 10: The Angle of Distortion

Very often, just increased **awareness** of these four barriers will reduce their negative impacts on organizational excellence, improvement or problem solving. But in addition, here are four related and helpful organizational norms or **values** that can help overcome these barriers:

- **We can very likely solve any problem we have the courage to discuss honestly.**

- **We need to discuss our problems with those who can contribute to solving them.**

- **Bosses, in particular, need to be sure they are getting honest upward feedback.**

- **Communication is not what is intended, but what is received (by others).**

Tough Times

A final word about communication in **difficult** situations. I've learned this from both the negative and positive aspects of my own experience as well as by observing others:

> Most of us have the skill or facility of being in **rapport** with another person. When we are tense, in disagreement or uncomfortable, we tend to move out of rapport at the very moment we most need it!

> By the way, being in rapport doesn't require agreement! It only requires evidence of rapport, such as: **respect, listening, visual attention, open-handed gestures and posture, and warmth in expression.**

I was recently asked by a client executive how he could improve his rapport with others. He had received some feedback that bosses, peers and subordinates found him difficult to work with. These suggestions helped him to become proactive in improving his relationships through rapport:

- Ask a respected third party to seek and collect **specific** feedback for you from others.

- Carefully study others (colleagues, clients, friends, family) who seem to be appreciated and effective.

- Capture yourself on video camera during some event that is long enough for you to forget to be self-conscious.

CHAPTER 16

SECRETS OF PROJECT MANAGEMENT

A growing number of firms are discovering that an effective project management (PM) process is vital for successful projects and in turn ... satisfied clients and prospering as a firm.

Firms as diverse as Hixson Architects & Engineers, McKinsey Management Consultants, Black & Veatch, and CH2M HILL place a very heavy emphasis on excellence in project management. These are some of their PM secrets:

1. The **Project** is considered to be the primary "profit center." Cost and other performance data is reviewed for units such as departments, divisions, regions, branches or cost centers as usual. However, **Projects** are the main focus for careful pricing, budgeting and review, and for the management of resources and costs (and profits in the private sector).

2. **Many people** in the organization may perform the project management functions, including project engineers/architects/ designers/scientists and others.

3. **Project Management** has a spectrum of competence and ability that spans from apprenticeship to mastery, like so:

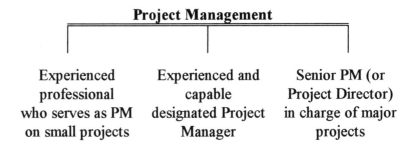

Project Management

| Experienced professional who serves as PM on small projects | Experienced and capable designated Project Manager | Senior PM (or Project Director) in charge of major projects |

4. **PM responsibilities** include critical activities like the following which are typical for a consulting or design firm:

   - Pre-planning the project proposal to meet the client's stated needs.

   - Careful, thorough, up-front dialogue with the client, to be certain we understood all their needs and expectations.

- Negotiating and contracting for adequate budget, schedule, risk transfer and compensation.

- Planning the project by logical tasks for the project team's needs.

- Organizing for the efficient use and consideration of human, financial and material resources in reaching predetermined project objectives.

- Developing the project team's communication, synergy and teamwork.

- Directing group action toward the achievement of the project objectives.

- Regularly reviewing the project with and for the client and key team members, for staying on track and without "surprises."

- Ensuring technical excellence in the project; meeting both client needs and appropriate standards.

- Controlling scope, quality, budget, schedule and assuring client satisfaction.

- Financial management for proper billing, collection and project profitability.

- Marketing the next project by performance, client rapport and project results.

- Project critique (for learnings and completion) and wrap-up.

5. Project managers' success at fulfilling such (clear) responsibilities are **tracked** by their senior management, in order to ...

- provide coaching and/or help, when needed.

- re-direct or influence the project, before problems become crises.

- recognize and reward strong performance by PMs.

- note **systemic** PM problems that need attention (TQM).

6. Senior management makes clear to all staff that their support to PMs is essential to having successful projects and satisfied clients.

One practical example of this is a Midwestern firm that makes it **easy** for PMs to provide performance feedback to departmental management for all technical and support staff who work on their projects.

7.   The organization **shows** that it regards designated project managers very highly in various ways:

   - In most cases, PMs are also principals, partners, associates, even vice presidents.

   - PMs are shown in the organization chart or scheme as functionally important (relative to other roles).

   - Successful PMs are provided with substantial financial rewards, based on project goals and project **performance**.

   - Unsuccessful PMs are not given new projects to mis-manage, but are removed or re-assigned to work they can do well.

8.   Project managers are provided with very **accurate and timely** project cost (or effort) reporting by the accounting staff.

   - Several firms provide PM consulting help on call from the accounting staff; experienced people who really **help**.

   - One Southeastern firm has met its goal of monthly project cost updates completed within 3 days of the month (or period) end.

   - Several firms provide on-line (computer) cost status for PMs, providing "printouts" only on request.

9.   Specialized support functions, such as ...

   - Marketing (help with proposals, presentations, negotiations, etc.)

   - Human Resources (help with special skills or overloads or new locations, etc.)

   - Legal (help with risk assessment, contract review, claims, etc.)

   - Accounting (help with cost database, project cost status, billings, collections, etc.)

These support functions are rewarded to the extent that they treat PMs as their **clients** to be supported and assisted (TQM). These special functions are encouraged to frequently seek feedback from PMs and others they serve, as to "how they're doing."

10. Senior management realizes that **one** problem project can wreck an organization's performance for a year, or conceivably put it out of business. They recognize that clients generally appreciate honest and prompt responses to problems. And so, problems get attention and specialized help quickly!

PM Flow Charts

A small but growing number of firms are flow-charting their project delivery or PM process as an effective way to define the project path, critical events and relationships. When the flow-charting becomes complex in a certain area such as negotiating, they may provide a sub-process flow chart. A sample (and simple) flow chart is shown in **Figure 11** (following).

PM "Training"

In spite of the large number of generic or general PM how-to books on the market, some firms are finding they need their own. Yet many firms have found their own PM manual is **ignored** after working so hard to produce it.

Several innovative organizations have found a way to help solve this problem! They go through these simple (but not easy) steps:

- Have 4 to 6 excellent PMs write a PM Guide (book) first draft.

- Convene a workshop of up to 35 PMs and other managers, to critique it in detail, in a carefully planned agenda.

- Revise the Guide based on the critique, and re-issue it, with thanks to all who helped.

- Maintain the Guide's currency by frequent updates and re-issues.

(Do you see the "training" in here?)

Those firms who've used this approach have far better PM Guidebooks than you could ever buy or have a consultant write for you.

1.
- STAY IN CLOSE TOUCH WITH EXISTING CLIENTS.
- ASSIST IN IDENTIFYING PROJECTS/PROSPECTS.
- LEAD OR ASSIST IN PROPOSALS/RESPONSES TO RFP'S.

2.
- INVOLVE APPROPRIATE TECHNICAL STAFFS AND SUBS.
- DETERMINE INITIAL SCOPE OF WORK ALONG WITH BUDGET, FEES, TERMS, SCHEDULE, ETC.

3.
- LEAD/ASSIST IN PRESENTATION(S) TO CLIENT.
- LEAD/ASSIST IN NEGOTIATING SCOPE AND TERMS.
- LEAD/ASSIST IN CONTRACTING WITH CLIENT.

4.
- RE-DEFINE SCOPE OF WORK, BASED ON CONTRACT.
- ADVISE TECHNICAL STAFF AND SUB-CONSULTANTS.
- DEVELOP PROJECT TEAM AND PROCEDURES.

5.
- INITIATE WORK ON PROJECT OBJECTIVES.
- PROPOSE STUDIES/DESIGN DECISIONS TO CLIENTS.
- MANAGE WORK AS TO SCOPE, COST, SCHEDULE.

6.
- REVIEW PROGRESS/DOCUMENTS WITH CLIENT.
- MANAGE AND NEGOTIATE SCOPE CHANGES.
- ASSURE PROJECT COORDINATION AND QUALITY.

7.
- MAINTENANCE MARKETING WITH CLIENT.
- ASSURE DOCUMENT DELIVERY ON SCHEDULE.
- TEND TO CLIENT BILLINGS AND COLLECTIONS.

8.
- MANAGE CONSTRUCTION PHASE SERVICES.
- CLOSE-OUT OF PROJECT; DOCUMENT DISPOSITION.
- POST-PROJECT REVIEW WITH CLIENT.

Figure 11: Typical Project Management Flow Chart

Changing PM Practices

Even after the best training and written resources, firms sometimes find that their PM practices are "stuck" in ways they'd like to change. Realizing that this may require a culture change, here are some other approaches to improving PM practices:

- Seek the strong support of senior management in making effective PM a high priority for rewards and recognition.

- Pursue ISO 9000 certification, which will require staff to know and follow the resulting written PM practices.

- Pursue TQM practices in the firm or agency (or division), and make improving the PM process an early priority and focus TQM efforts on that.

- When tempted to do a "structural re-organization," consider redirecting that same improvement effort, energy and money into assessing and improving project management.

- When growth or attrition provide hiring opportunities, look for the best possible experienced outside candidates to fill PM positions.

CHAPTER 17

MEETINGS THAT REALLY WORK!

For all of our complaints about meetings, and they are getting louder, it seems that ...

- meetings are needed more than ever.
- TQM hasn't helped much here, if at all.
- they are still essential to daily work.

Rich Millet of Woodward-Clyde recently found a little book on meetings that was very helpful. It looked vaguely familiar. I noticed it was first published in 1976! It's *How to Make Meetings Work* by Michael Doyle and David Strauss (Jove Books, New York). It's still a great resource.

Meetings can be a group's best work ... or its worst. They can increase teamwork ... or fray relationships. Meetings can save time ... or waste expensive hours. **Poor** meetings almost always grow out of problems like these:

- **Purpose** or objectives of the meeting aren't clear.
- **Information** is missing or people aren't prepared.
- **Sub-groups** aren't used to draft recommendations or proposals.
- **Process** of the meeting isn't guided by leader/moderator.
- **Organization** of the work is lacking or ignored.
- **Record** of discussion or decisions isn't developed.

Check 'Em Out

One way to make meetings work is to evaluate them often. The following **rating factors** will help you both rate and **continuously improve** work meetings.

To what extent am I/are we satisfied with:	**1 (Low) 5 (High)**
1. How we're using our time on our topics and needs?	_____
2. How "air time" is used among our group members?	_____
3. The amount and clarity of factual data and information available?	_____

4. Our openness about our feelings, opinions and hunches?   _____

5. Our decision making processes as appropriate to the topic at hand?   _____

6. Our agenda development, management and follow-up?   _____

7. Our meeting moderator/leader or task manager?   _____

8. Our meeting facilitator(s) as they help with our process?   _____

9. Our meeting recorder as he/she tracks our work?   _____

10. Our ability to disagree openly and productively on issues?   _____

Other needs for effective and productive meetings:

- Room shape, size, furnishings are adequate.

- Ambient temperature and ventilation are satisfactory.

- Chart pad or other visual aids are available to use.

- "Outside" concerns (illness, family, finances) aren't interfering.

Questions that may help us get unstuck:

- What are we doing now?

- How does it feel to me?

- What do I want or need now?

- What do we need less or more of?

- What issue are we avoiding?

One very simple, fast and effective way to improve meetings of all kinds is to ask participants to help list the following:

- What were the "plusses" (things that went well)?

- What were the "deltas" (things needing change)?

Meeting Leadership

TQM and other forms of organization development are requiring more sophisticated meeting leadership. Here is an effective approach to assuring things go well:

Key Roles for Effective Meetings

- **Leader Responsibilities**

   To **lead** the group in its **work on tasks**, so its mission is most effectively accomplished and in a way that cultivates teamwork.

   And, to share leadership tasks with others in the group when appropriate.

- **Recorder Responsibilities**

   To **capture** the key points of the group's work **during its work** in visible ways that will enable people to be maximally effective, as well as follow-up documentation after the group's work is done.

   And, to ask for help with the Recorder tasks, when necessary.

- **Facilitator Responsibilities**

   To **observe and help** with the group's **process** as it works, assisting as needed to help achieve group task accomplishment and team development through process awareness.

   And, to help and support the group leader and recorder whenever possible.

- **Member Responsibilities**

   To participate in the group's work, contributing whatever the group needs from its members at the moment ...

   - ideas
   - facts
   - feelings
   - observations
   - analysis
   - reflection
   - discussion
   - decision
   - action
   - review

What's a Consensus?

Teams these days seem to get hung up on wanting consensus decision-making for most issues. This problem has two parts:

- **First**, not all issues or topics are **worth** the time and energy of working to consensus.
- **Second**, consensus **doesn't** require unanimity or agreement by all members.

Generally, the team will have a sense of which issues are worth their discussion time and the leader need only ask the team if in doubt.

When the team **does** want to work toward consensus, here are some helpful guidelines that define "consensus":

- A decision-making process which gives all team members a chance to be **heard**.
- A process which **tries** to meet the needs or concerns of all team members.
- A discussion of **pros and cons** of different options.
- As close as the team can get to **agreement** prior to action.
- A decision that all team members can and will **support**.

Staff Meetings: You Need Two Kinds

Executives and managers often find that **"communication"** is both their biggest problem, their biggest job and biggest opportunity as well. Much of it, maybe **most** of it, can be handled by means of two different kinds of staff meetings.

One-to-One Meetings are for and with **each** of the boss's staff members, at a time of mutual convenience. This is the **staff member's** meeting, to cover **his/her** agenda, and to ...

- review general progress on major projects.
- raise problems or needs for help or consultation.
- keep his/her manager informed as necessary.
- present his/her staff and their project work (one at a time).

These meetings can be at either person's office, but probably some meetings need to get the boss out of his/her office to improve management visibility and to keep in touch with people.

Staff Team Meetings are for **all** the boss's **direct** reports, at a time of mutual convenience, for a period of an hour or two. The goals of **this** meeting are usually ...

- general information exchange.

- project or program coordination.

- team planning and problem-solving.

- team members serving as consultants to one another.

Electronic Communication

I debated whether or not to include a section on the need to aggressively use technology, and decided managers already do that very well!

Faxes, E-mail, voice mail, cellular phones and teleconferencing have greatly improved our **ability** to communicate quickly and over long distances. Unfortunately, they have also reduced real communication in some cases. Here's why we think so:

- Fewer meetings with face-to-face discussions.

- Avoiding, forgetting or postponing incoming "mail."

- Over-reliance on non-personal communication; too little "management by walking around."

Increasingly, people complain that their manager spends way too much time sitting glued to his/her computer, out of touch with the real work and staff. And this is said of managers at all levels in organizations.

While we must use technology to the maximum for competitive cost effectiveness, we must also maintain essential human contact (high tech requires high touch)!

CHAPTER 18

STRENGTHENING THE STAFFING FUNCTION

Our experience and field research in assisting our clients suggests that their recruiting and selection processes often lead to serious mistakes in hiring.

Managers and leaders often spend too much time worrying about compensation instead of taking the time required to do excellent selection work.

Perhaps 50% of experienced hires and even 30% of promotions don't work out well, and need some sort of remedial action within a year or two.

Following are some thoughts that may improve these awful odds in terms of hiring, developing, promoting and keeping good people.

Get Ready!

Try to visualize where we may need people before we actually do and be on the lookout for people with those skills.

- Develop key responsibilities and/or objectives for each open position.

- Use many sources to find strong candidates, including networking, referrals, searches, advertising, campus contacts, recent hires, etc.

- Analyze the "success attributes" of our currently effective staff.

Be Realistic

Select people for their strengths (that we need), while avoiding costly weaknesses.

- Look at enough candidates; don't settle for "almost OK."

- Look at what people **have** done; it's the surest guide to what they **will** do.

- Be mindful of candidates' **attitudes**; they are as important as skills and experiences, and harder to change.

- Use many interviews for each strong candidate and compare the results of different interviews and interviewers.

Interview Well

Avoid the most common interviewing errors made by managers as they meet with candidates. Here are some we see most often:

- Making snap judgments in the first 5-10 minutes of the interview.

- Wasting time reviewing what we should already know from the résumé.

- Talking too much, asking too little and listening too little.

- Not making notes of key points we hear and need to recall.

- Being too polite to ask some "hard questions" related to challenges faced, problems solved, situations similar to ours.

- Not looking for people potentially better than we are, while avoiding clones of ourselves or people who are "pleasers."

Develop People

Recognize that the job and situation provides more real development than "training" ever will.

- Be sure that the first assignment for inexperienced hires is well selected; it's a crucial developmental experience.

- Provide a stimulating, challenging work environment.

- Know who are among our best recruiters, interviewers, coaches and mentors, and use them well in those vital functions.

- Have an aggressive development system so we can promote from within.

- Provide for honest, timely, clear, descriptive, constructive performance feedback ...

    - to managers from their staffs.

    - to individuals from their manager.

    - from internal and external clients to everyone.

Motivate People

Motivate and muscle-build staff whenever productivity, creativity, morale and teamwork are low, by ...

    - recognizing strong performers.

    - dropping poor performers.

- Use periods of low workload to drop lowest performers rather than use up financial reserves.

- Have fewer people than "needed" but reward them well for their efforts.

- Pay well but pay for performance; see that highest performers are highest paid. This is easiest with an incentive compensation system to supplement salaries.

Other Key Points

- Don't promote on "potential" but rather on demonstrated abilities **already** showing up in the individual's work.

- Strive for deep "bench strength" where there is at least one, maybe two candidates being developed for each key position.

- Involve people in tasks that develop the organization **and** the individual at the same time, such as ...

    - process improvement teams.

    - strategic planning committees.

    - corrective action teams.

    - product or service development.

- Provide lots of **effective** training for what are often called "people skills," like these:

    - Basic communication skills.

    - Team problem-solving skills.

    - Team, leader, facilitator, recorder.

Interesting Questions for Job Interviews

Clients tell us they get more interest from job candidates when interviewers really dig and try to learn about each candidate. Candidates also respect interviewers' efforts to avoid mistakes in hiring because it hurts the candidates the most!

Here are some of the most useful questions we've gleaned over the years while trying to help our clients learn more from interviews:

- What do you want in your **ideal job**? (Listen for their criteria and goals.)

- What **appeals** to you about this job you're applying for? (Listen for hopes and concerns.)

- Why did you choose your **present** (or last) job? (Listen for a preference for freedom and options, or procedures and structure, benefits and perks, environment, and so forth.)

- Tell me about a work experience that was particularly **successful**. (Listen for "I," "me and others." Was it a solo or team effort?)

- What did you **like** about that experience? (Listen for an interest in working with things or people or both.)

- Tell me about a project or situation that gave you **trouble**. (Listen for coping strategies, persistence, use of resources.)

- Why would you (or did you) **leave** your present employer? (Listen for blaming others, looking for responsibility or ease, and so on.)

- How do you **know** you've done a good job? (Listen for internal vs. external standards of performance, or some of both.)

- What **challenges** do you see in this job you are applying for? (Listen for confidence or lack of it, perceptual ability and strategic skills.)

- Here's a **challenge** you may face in this job (describe a **real** challenge). How would you handle it?

- Here's **another** challenge you may face in this job (describe another **real** challenge). How would you tackle this one?

- Tell me about one or two particular **accomplishments** from your last several years of life, either work-related or personal, that you feel comfortable telling me.

These kinds of questions can really get a candidate "warmed-up" to his/her topic and they may go on and on or give too much detail. So, feel free to interrupt or redirect the candidate; neither of you wants to waste precious interview time.

Final Thoughts

Robert Wendover has written a brief, clear and helpful book: ***Smart Hiring: The Complete Guide for Recruiting Employees*** (published by Management Staff Press, Inc., 1989). This great little reference covers everything from nepotism to immigration in matters of employment.

Successful recruiting, selection and hiring is about the most important time that managers and leaders can spend. The results of their work in this will either bless or bedevil their organization for years to come!

CHAPTER 19

MANAGERS HAVE TO BE FACILITATORS

We are rapidly becoming aware of the need for and benefits of "facilitators" in all kinds of organizations.

Many firms that are pursuing Total Quality Management or Re-engineering in any of their various forms are discovering the need for "facilitators." Strategic planning work also requires facilitators. In fact, **most any work meeting** would benefit from having **good** facilitators.

Facilitators provide key functions in enabling a group or team to start up, or to expand or continue effectiveness, whether on a single special task or project, or for ongoing work.

The function of a facilitator is described differently by various authors, ranging from process observer to meeting leader, but common to all definitions are these. Facilitators ...

- focus on **process**; on **how** the group is working.
- **listen** carefully and **use** what others say.
- assist the group in its **approaches** to planning, problem solving, and getting "unstuck."
- help the group improve its **collective** skills as it works.

> Our experience suggests that facilitation skills are increasingly important to managers and leaders anytime they work in a group setting!

Facilitators also support another key function, that of **recorder** (sometimes called scribe) of the group. The recorder's job is to see that the group's work is captured and made visible **as** it works, as well as after the work.

The group leader, recorder and facilitator form a "leadership team" for effective groups who exhibit teamwork, creativity, productivity and effective task completion, as described earlier in **Chapter 16**.

Facilitator Skills

Few references address facilitator skills. One of the few and one of the best is *How to Lead Work Teams* by Fran Rees (Pfeiffer & Company Publishers, 1991).

Excellent training in facilitator skills is offered by **Interaction Associates**, headquarters at 600 Townsend Street, Suite 550, San Francisco, California **94103**. Their workshops are offered in Boston and Dallas as well as San Francisco.

Over the years, we have developed a short list of the physical and mental skills necessary to being a useful, helpful facilitator of work groups and teams. Here, then, is the **bare minimum** list of facilitator skills for **managers and leaders**:

- Focus mostly on process (how we are working), not content (topics or issues).
- Stand or sit where you can see everyone.
- Speak clearly and slowly.
- Keep the meeting's objective in mind.
- Assist the group in amending the agenda.
- Remind the group of time and schedule, as needed.
- Listen carefully enough to paraphrase contributors.
- Solicit clarification when the message is not clear.
- Encourage the total group to participate.
- Avoid being judgmental about contributors.
- Acknowledge the ownership of ideas.
- Notice tangents and help the group get back on track.
- Look for signs of teamwork, leadership, fatigue or disinterest, energy and excitement.
- Challenge the group when necessary.
- Support individuals when they need it.
- **Ask the group for help when you need it.**
- Suggest a list of action items for follow-up after the meeting.
- Suggest a brief evaluation of the meeting; perhaps plusses and needed changes.

Other Important Abilities

- Develop an understanding of **task** and **maintenance** roles: Task is moving the group forward, and maintenance is nurturing teamwork and relationships.
- Sense when it's most effective to use **large** and **small** groups:
  - **Large** groups are best for data gathering, brainstorming, voting or choosing, and reviewing a draft proposal.

- **Subgroups** are best for allowing more free air time, doing a study, defining or analyzing a problem, and developing a draft or proposal.

• Develop several ways to help the group **choose** high-priority items from a long list (of anything):

- Approval voting: Each member votes for all items he or she supports or wants. Tally the votes.

- *N/3* method: Each member gets the number of votes equal to one-third of the total items in the list. Tally the votes.

- Lobbying: Each member lobbies (speaks for) his or her favorite items, for no more than 1 minute per person at a time. Let consensus emerge.

• Develop skill in using several **group** problem-solving aids or guides such as the following four.

Group Problem-Solving Tools

After years of working with management and executive groups, boards, steering committees and quality teams, four "tools" seem to emerge as the most useful for group use.

Facilitators, leaders and managers need to be or become comfortable in the use of these four simple tools in **Table 6** to assure that groups they help or lead are as **effective** as they need to be.

Table 6: Four Group Problem Solving Tools

Tool	Purpose	Resources	Watchouts
Brainstorming	Creatively listing all possible: • problems • causes • symptoms • solutions	Easel and chart pad Clearly focused statement of the **point** to be addressed by the group Recorder Leader	Rule 1 is: **No criticism** Most groups unconsciously begin to criticize Shy people may need to go in "rotation" (make it OK to pass)

Tool	Purpose	Resources	Watchouts
Displayed Thinking	Organizing items (ideas) by broad type or category ... • causes • factors • aspects and so on	Easel and chart pad or 3x5 cards and tape Identification of broad types or **categories** to be used Recorder Leader	Sometimes the broad categories need adjustment so the 3x5 cards are easier to use It's only an aid to brainstorming by creating categories
Pareto Analysis (by group)	Establishing the amount or frequency for the various types of ... • problems • causes • occurrences in a particular situation	Easel and chart pad Identification of items to be checked **Data** collected from the work situation by someone Recorder Leader	It only sounds complicated It's actually the simplest kind of analysis Oftentimes, it doesn't even need to be numeric to be useful
Flow-Charting (by group)	Determining the actual steps in a work process in order to ... • understand it • identify glitches • improve on it, or • re-engineer it	3x5 or 4x6 Post-It-Notes or cards and tape and markers Smooth wall to work on, or Chart sheets taped to the wall Recorder Leader	Important to have all functions represented in group Needs time for discussion and consensus Needs to be verified by others who use/do it, before improving it

CHAPTER 20

RELATIONSHIPS THAT GET RESULTS

Managers, leaders, executives and supervisors are often frustrated by their inability to **get results through others**. Most of the time we are likely to feel or believe this difficulty is caused by the other person (or group).

In many cases, the cause is simply the **way** we are approaching the other person (or group).

We all tend to fall into habitual ways of directing, coaching, requesting or assigning. We are usually oblivious as to **how** we approach others. We need to consider two practical truisms here:

- Trying the same failed approach over and over will **not** yield better results.
- People and situations differ widely and one approach will **not** suit all circumstances.

We may get some help from "systems theory," first noted by the biologist Von Bertelanfy in his observation of systems in nature. Here are a few relevant elements of "systems theory":

- Parts of a system are not independent; a change in one will cause a **change in others**.
- The part of a system with the most flexibility (the most options or choices) has the most power to **succeed or survive**.

Relationships Make Things Happen

Every person has a **relationship** that "connects" him/her with other people. Working relationships may be good or poor, positive or negative, productive or dysfunctional. It doesn't matter, so long as a relationship **exists**.

In **Figure 12** (following) persons A and B have a relationship. That relationship has a **history** which may be ... long or short, superficial or intense. The relationship has a **quality** which may be ... good or poor, personal or professional.

Here are some things we can conclude with the help of systems theory:

- Person A **cannot** change person B directly.
- Person A **can** change person A (who then becomes A').
- If A's change is visible, observable and credible to B, then ...
- Person B **will** change in response to person A's change!
- B's change is not particularly predictable, but may be in the direction hoped for by A.

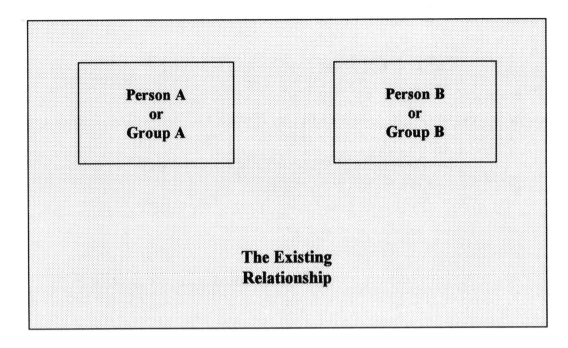

Figure 12: Relationships Create a System

Practical Samples

Examples from real work organizations are plentiful. You could identify many for yourself. Here are several we've noted:

- A supervisor who is normally pretty critical of a staff member, begins to acknowledge his/her employee's contributions, to give a little recognition instead of focusing only on flaws.

- An engineer who frequently helps a colleague (who requests a lot of help), makes a change. Rather than continuing, or just saying "no," she directs the colleague to the technical reference files for help.

- A manager who usually ignores a chronic complainer, asks him/her instead to develop practical suggestions to address a particular complaint, offering the complainer the chance to be a problem solver.

Barriers

So, if this process is so easy, why don't we see it or use it much more often? As "person A" we may not try something as simple, but radical, as this because ...

- we don't want to change any of our own behaviors.

94

- we don't want to appear to be the cause of B's present behavior.

- we may feel they (B) ought to change because we "say so."

- we prefer trying the same old comfortable things that haven't worked before!

Groups Too?

Does the same process work where A and B are **groups** instead of people? **Yes!** In fact, either A or B may be a person or a group. The only differences to expect are these:

- Group A may have more difficulty agreeing on initiating change, or what change to make.

- Group B may require more time to verify that A's change is real and trustworthy.

Principles of Positive Reinforcement

"Positive Reinforcement" has been around a long time but isn't often well used. The interesting fact is, positive and **negative** reinforcement operate **all the time**, whether we are conscious of that or not! Here are some principles we need to be **conscious** of:

- That which is recognized or even acknowledged will be **repeated**.

- Recognition or acknowledgment need not be often and **should not** be predictable (as in "always").

- **Specific** feedback (positive or negative) is more valuable and performance-motivating than general feedback.

- Recognition or acknowledgment **often** needs to be private (one to one) to avoid jealousy or embarrassment.

- Criticism or negative feedback **always** needs to be private (one to one) even if it is for all members of a group (for example: To all Project Managers).

- Extinction (doing/saying nothing) is often effective at **removing** behavior. This applies equally to behaviors you want and don't want!

- Criticism or negative feedback **is** necessary. However, it attaches a negative stigma to the giver in the eyes of the receiver if it's over-used.

- Consequently, criticism or negative feedback needs to be private, helpfully offered and given as a small percentage of total feedback.

    - Rule of thumb: 10 positive to 1 negative.

- "Sandwich" feedback (a negative and a positive; or positive, negative, positive) is ineffective. Avoid using this technique that has been popularized in past personnel articles.

- Criticism or negative feedback is most helpful when it gives all this information:

    - What happened, as you saw it?

    - What were the impacts on you and others?

    - What would be better next time?

- It is possible to change work performance dramatically by using positive reinforcement alone. It's even more effective to use a little, well-conceived criticism up to 10% of the time.

Based on work by ...

- David W. Thompson in *Managing People: Influencing Behavior* (C.V. Mosby Co., 1978).

- Aubrey C. Daniels in *Bringing Out the Best in People* (McGraw-Hill, Inc., 1994).

- Mel and Carol Hensey from our consulting practice.

CHAPTER 21

LEADING "UNMANAGEABLE" SYSTEMS

On occasion, our clients are churches, professional and trade associations, charitable organizations and universities ... which have an important difference compared to other institutions:

They are essentially VOLUNTEER by nature!

Whoa, you may say ... how are universities VOLUNTEER? Aren't people paid for their work? Well, yes they are. But many faculty are tenured, which means that except for a minimal teaching load, they may do as they please with regard to meetings, service, research, and so on.

Lately, we came upon yet another situation which functions like a VOLUNTEER organization. Our client, director of an R&D division, has been creatively influencing technical people who are **not** in his division, to be more proactive in sharing technology and assistance across the firm. He was frustrated at the slow rate of interest and progress.

Then, we noticed that this too is essentially a VOLUNTEER effort on everyone's part. Viewed in this new light, the effort **is** successful.

Other Organizations

Even in the era of downsizing, outplacement, dropping wages and benefits, foreign competition, dislocation and migration, most American workers are "different."

Compared to many other countries, American workers of all kinds increasingly expect to be treated with respect and consideration. If they aren't, they'll not do their best! And, they may eventually even leave.

As a result, many managers have found there's a need to lead people as if they are **"volunteers"** in most kinds of organizations, even including the military!

Leading "Volunteers"

It seems to us that one of the most important differences between **leading** and **managing** is this ...

Leading requires gaining the commitment of others to a task or course of action because they've become convinced it's what **they** want to do!

Apologies to President (then General) Eisenhower, who said it more simply and elegantly.

Gaining that commitment from others when you lack ... or prefer not to use ... coercive power, is the important essence of leading "volunteers" in whatever kind of organization, situation or system.

Here are some of the more productive ways to gain that commitment in others ...

- **Involve** them in the discussions of goals, alternatives, benefits, etc.

- **Demonstrate** your own commitment in actions as well as communication.

- **Point out** the common overarching goals, appealing to self-interest.

- Since money probably isn't available or isn't a factor, provide **other** meaningful rewards:

    - Acknowledgment.

    - Peer recognition.

    - Simple, tangible awards that can be used, worn or displayed.

    - Total team recognition.

    - Sincere praise for work unusually well done.

    - A special treat or opportunity.

- Review progress without criticism. People will criticize themselves.

- Make a part of each meeting or gathering rewarding in some way, perhaps with donuts or pizza, a small book or a tape ... people love to snack and like to learn.

A broader strategy could be to learn from the **leaders** of **effective volunteer** organizations such as the Red Cross, Girl Scouts, Big Brothers, the Prison Fellowship, hospital candy stripers (volunteers in service), blood drive organizations, volunteer board members, and so on.

CHAPTER 22

USING THE PAST AS FUTURE GUIDE

Three "futurists" have studied the past specifically to give us some guideposts for successfully coping with the current turbulent change as we move into the future.

JOEL BARKER studied the "power of vision" in the past for nations, people and children, and then presented these highlights in his video *The Power of Vision* ...

- Vision must be initiated by the leadership group.

- Values provide guidance for the vision development.

- To engage others, a vision should be positive and inspiring.

- It needs to be shared and supported by the vision community.

- The vision will be most useful when it's specific and detailed.

IMPARATO AND HARARI looked at 3000 years of human history and found only two other epochs as turbulent as ours. In *Jumping the Curve*, they suggest we ...

- Look, think and plan a customer (or client) ahead.

- Build our systems around the customer(s) and our organization around our systems.

- Reward best those staff who live the values and meet the goals of our organization.

- Consider really making customers the ultimate judges of quality.

As we've worked with several client firms and agencies, they and we have discovered that Barker, Imparato and Harari provide us with some useful implications for the future (**Table 7**).

Table 7: Some Implications
for Service Businesses, Agencies, Associations, Institutions

STAFFING AND HUMAN RESOURCES	<ul><li>When hiring, find the best people available.</li><li>Keep a core team of key staff stable over time.</li><li>Supplement them with **talented** temporaries.</li><li>Help all to understand "Marketing" is part of the job.</li><li>Develop Partnerships with suppliers and "competitors."</li></ul>

Table 7 (continued):
Some Implications for Service Businesses, Agencies, Associations, Institutions

FINANCIAL SUCCESS NEEDS	• Set clear and specific financial goals and/or budgets. • Fix under-performing ... staff, units, customers, partners. • Price services based on **value** whenever possible. • Develop effective and timely cost-tracking systems. • Don't wait for the "good times"; they're here!
SERVICE TECHNOLOGY AND INFORMATION TECHNOLOGY	• Have or develop top-notch technical people in each service area. • Develop services niches that provide true customer value. • Use networked PC's (computers) to facilitate E-mail, computer-conferencing, common databases, GIS, and the rest. • Benchmark the technology and customer service leaders in **any** business or service. • Bring in experienced hires from successful organizations.

MARKETING AND CLIENT RELATIONS	• Be clear about who are the A, B and C clients, where ...
	  - A's - want to work as partners.
	  - B's - are generally easy to serve well.
	  - C's - are difficult, requiring special procedures.
	• Develop ever stronger skills in listening to clients.
	• Use creative approaches such as Maister's "reverse seminars" where a key client is invited to talk to staff about their needs.
	• Recognize the usefulness of client problems as opportunities to serve and "sell" as well.
	• Find new needs to address (before others do).

OPERATIONS AND SERVICE DELIVERY	• Establish procedures with flow charts rather than manuals. • Slowly but surely learn and apply TQM concepts and tools. • Encourage staff to be continually developing/improving processes and skills. • Cross-train and broaden skills; develop staff flexibility. • For project-related services, develop able project managers.

REFERENCES AND RESOURCES

Books

At America's Service by Karl Albrecht, published by Dow Jones Irwin, Homewood, IL, 1988.

Benchmarking for Best Practices by C.E. Bogen and M.J. English, published by McGraw-Hill, Inc., New York, NY, 1994.

Bringing out the Best in People by Aubrey C. Daniels, published by McGraw-Hill, Inc., 1994.

Collective Excellence: Building Effective Teams by Mel Hensey, published by the American Society of Civil Engineers (ASCE), New York, NY, 1992.

Future Shock by Alvin Tofler, published by Random House, New York, NY, 1970.

Generation to Generation by Edwin H. Freidman, published by Guilford Press, New York, NY, 1985.

Hound of Heaven, a poem by Francis Thompson, published by Dodd, Mead, New York, NY, 1922.

How to Lead Work Teams by Fran Rees, Pfeiffer and Co. Publishers, San Diego, CA, 1991.

How to Make Meetings Work by Michael Doyle and David Strauss, published by Wyden Books, New York, NY, 1976.

Implementing TQM; Revised Second Edition, by Joseph Jablonski, published by Technical Management Consortium, Inc., Albuquerque, NM, 1994.

Inside the Technical Consulting Business by Harvey Kaye; a Wiley-Interscience Publication, New York, NY, 1986.

Jumping the Curve by Nicholas Imparato and Oren Harari, published by Jossey-Bass, Inc., San Francisco, CA, 1993.

Leading Teams: Mastering the New Role by Zenger-Miller, published by Business One Irwin, 1993.

Lincoln on Leadership by Donald T. Phillips, published by Warner Books, New York, NY, 1992.

Making Quality Work by Labovitz, Chang and Rosansky, published by Harper Business Division of Harper Collins Publishers, New York, NY, 1993.

Managing as a Performing Art by Peter Vaill, published by Jossey-Bass, Inc., San Francisco, CA, 1989.

Managing People: Influencing Behavior by David W. Thompson, published by C.V. Mosby Co., St. Louis, MO, 1978.

Next Operation as Customer (NOAC) by Keki Bhote, published by American Management Association (AMACOM), New York, NY, 1991.

Overcoming Organizational Defenses by Chris Argyris, published by Prentice-Hall, a division of Simon & Schuster, Inc., Inglewood Cliff, NJ, 1990.

Partnering for Success by Thomas R. Warne, published by the American Society of Civil Engineers (ASCE), New York, NY, 1994.

Problem Bosses by Mardy Grothe and Peter Wylie, published by Facts on File, New York, NY, 1987.

Re-engineering the Corporation by Michael Hammer and James Champy, published by Harper Business, New York, NY, 1993.

Servant Leadership by Robert K. Greenleaf, published by Paulist Press, New York, NY, 1977.

Smart Hiring: The Complete Guide for Recruiting Employees by Robert Wendover, published by Management Staff Press, Inc., 1989.

The "I Hate Selling" Book by Allan S. Boress, published by American Management Association (AMACOM), New York, NY, 1995.

The Team Building Tool Kit: Tips, Tactics and Rules for Effective Workplace Teams by Deborah Harrington-Mackin, published by American Management Association (AMACOM), New York, NY, 1994.

The Team Handbook by Peter R. Scholtes and other contributors, published by Joiner Associates, Inc., 3800 Regent Street, Madison, WI, 1990.

Articles

Partnering to Save Troubled Projects, an article by Jim Brown, published in the *Journal of Management in Engineering*, by the American Society of Civil Engineers (ASCE), New York, NY, May/June, 1994.

Re-Engineering in Action: A Manufacturing Institute Conference, an article by Tim Davis, published in the *Planning Review*, by the Planning Forum, Oxford, OH, July/August, 1993.

Re-Engineering Work: Don't Automate, Obliterate, an article by Michael Hammer, published in the *Harvard Business Review*, by the Graduate School of Business Administration, Harvard University, Boston, MA, July/August, 1990 .

The Boss Has Read Another New Book, published in the *Management Review*, by American Management Association (AMACOM), New York, NY, 1994.

Journals and Publications

Business Week, published by McGraw-Hill, New York, NY.

Construction Industry Institute, published by The University of Texas at Austin, College of Engineering, Austin, TX.

Engineering News Record (ENR), published by McGraw-Hill, New York, NY.

Harvard Business Review, published by the Graduate School of Business Administration, Harvard University, Boston, MA.

Journal of Management in Engineering, published by the American Society of Civil Engineers (ASCE), New York, NY.

Management Review, published by American Management Association (AMACOM), New York, NY.

Planning Review, published by the Planning Forum, Oxford, OH.

Professional Services Management Journal (PSMJ), Newton, MA.

Quality by Design, a Quality Management Newsletter for Architects, Engineers and Constructors, published by William M. Hayden, Jr. Consultants, Inc., Jacksonville, FL.

INDEX